KINDNESS
IS GOOD
FOR YOU

DAVID R. HAMILTON PhD

HAY HOUSE

Australia • Canada • Hong Kong • India
South Africa • United Kingdom • United States

First published and distributed in the United Kingdom by:
Hay House UK Ltd, 292B Kensal Rd, London W10 5BE.
Tel.: (44) 20 8962 1230; Fax: (44) 20 8962 1239. www.hayhouse.co.uk

Published and distributed in the United States of America by:
Hay House, Inc., PO Box 5100, Carlsbad, CA 92018-5100.
Tel.: (1) 760 431 7695 or (800) 654 5126;
Fax: (1) 760 431 6948 or (800) 650 5115. www.hayhouse.com

Published and distributed in Australia by:
Hay House Australia Ltd, 18/36 Ralph St, Alexandria NSW 2015.
Tel.: (61) 2 9669 4299; Fax: (61) 2 9669 4144. www.hayhouse.com.au

Published and distributed in the Republic of South Africa by:
Hay House SA (Pty), Ltd, PO Box 990, Witkoppen 2068.
Tel./Fax: (27) 11 467 8904. www.hayhouse.co.za

Published and distributed in India by:
Hay House Publishers India, Muskaan Complex, Plot No.3, B-2, Vasant Kunj,
New Delhi – 110 070. Tel.: (91) 11 4176 1620; Fax: (91) 11 4176 1630.
www.hayhouse.co.in

Distributed in Canada by:
Raincoast, 9050 Shaughnessy St, Vancouver, BC V6P 6E5.
Tel.: (1) 604 323 7100; Fax: (1) 604 323 2600

A catalogue record for this book is available from the British Library.

ISBN 978-1-84850-178-2

Printed in the UK by CPI William Clowes Ltd, Beccles, NR34 7TL.

All of the papers used in this product are recyclable, and made from wood
grown in managed, sustainable forests and manufactured at mills certified to

ISO 14001 and/or EMAS.

I dedicate this book to the people who have shown me the most kindness and most helped create the environment of love and support that I needed to become a writer and public speaker:

To Elizabeth for her constant love, support, inspiration and encouragement.

To my mum, dad and three sisters, Lesley, Kerry and Lynn,

and to Elizabeth's parents, Elma and Peter,

for believing in me and always supporting me when I needed it.

'This is my simple religion. There is no need for temples; no need for complicated philosophy. Our own brain, our own heart is our temple; the philosophy is kindness.'

HH the Dalai Lama

CONTENTS

ACKNOWLEDGEMENTS

I have been on the receiving end of a lot of kindness in my life, the spirit of which was the undercurrent that inspired me to write this book and guided me along the way to its completion.

First I'd like to express my gratitude to my life partner, Elizabeth Caproni. If it hadn't been for Elizabeth's kindness, and her love, support and advice over the years, you would not be reading this book right now. She has been both my rock and the wind behind my sails.

I'd also like to express gratitude to my family – my mum, dad and three sisters – for always being supportive of me. When I made the decision a few years back to resign from my job in the pharmaceutical industry so that I could write and speak, they were all behind me and have continued to support me 100 per cent to this day.

I am grateful to Elizabeth's parents, Elma and Peter, for their many kindnesses towards me over the years and the belief that they have always had in me.

I'd like to express my thanks to the staff of Starbucks in Windsor for their support of my writing of this book and for the friendly and creative atmosphere that helped me to write it.

I'd also like to say thank you to the people who told me their stories of kindness. I am certain that their experiences will inspire and touch the hearts of many people.

I would like to thank my editor, Lizzie Hutchins. Lizzie has, once again, smoothed over the cracks in my writing and, at times, done a little bit of restructuring that has brought the book to its current high standard.

And I am grateful to Jonathan Pegg, of Jonathan Pegg Literary Agency, for kindly representing my interests while negotiating the publication of this book.

I am also grateful to the staff of Hay House in the UK. In particular, Michelle Pilley, Jo Burgess and Jo Lal have shown belief in my writing, and in me, and offered me expert guidance on a number of occasions. I'm grateful to Nicola Fletcher, too, and Adam Harvey, previously, for handling my monthly newsletters and ensuring that people around the world can read my articles. But I'm grateful to the entire staff, too, present and past, because together they help Hay House to be what it is: a publishing house with the unshakeable spirit of wishing to make the world a better place, a house that I am very proud to be published by.

And I would finally like to extend my gratitude to Louise Hay and Reid Tracy for sowing the seeds of Hay House and building it into what it is today, and also for believing in me and giving me the opportunity not only to be published in the USA but also to speak to US audiences.

INTRODUCTION

This book is about kindness. It contains up-to-date studies that show that kindness is good for your health, as well as stories to inspire you to put it into practice, which is where the benefits arise. As St Thomas Aquinas said, 'I would rather feel compassion than know the meaning of it.'

Compassion itself is also included in the book, because kindness grows out of it. We share another's pain, compassionately wish them free of suffering and are then motivated to help them and to be kind. I have also looked briefly at gratitude and forgiveness. Gratitude is a mark of being kind to life by being aware of all that is around us, and when we are grateful, we acknowledge the people and situations in our life and express thanks for them. Doing this is good for us, and so counting our blessings is actually a mark of kindness towards ourselves. Forgiveness is also a way of being kind to ourselves. It is a tool to set ourselves free.

When there is more kindness in the world, it will be better for all of us. So I hope that this combination of short stories of kindness *and* science will inspire you to perform more acts of kindness yourself.

To help you along the way, there are also a number of short exercises, as well as suggestions for healing or improving your relationships, increasing your social connectedness and being able to forgive.

You will learn from a large number of scientific studies in this book that kindness can make you happier. It can alleviate depression and improve your relationships. It is good for your heart and your immune system, and new studies are even showing that it helps you to live longer.

Compassion is similar in its benefits. And new discoveries around the 'nerve of compassion', the vagus nerve, suggest that compassion might play a much greater role in the maintenance of good health than previously thought, by reducing inflammation, which has a hand in many disease conditions, including heart disease and cancer.

Gratitude is also extremely health-giving. It alleviates depression, makes us happier, improves the quality of our relationships, is a good treatment for insomnia and can help us live longer. These are just some of the conclusions of a growing body of research in the field of positive psychology.

Forgiveness, too, is beneficial to our health. Studies now show that it significantly reduces hurt, anger, stress, anxiety and depression and gives us hope for the future. It is also good for the heart, as it reduces blood pressure and improves blood flow.

Having good-quality relationships is also good for our health. Good relationships are associated with a longer lifespan and a much lower risk of heart disease. People in good-quality relationships are, on the whole, healthier than those who are in poor-quality relationships or socially isolated. Part of this is due to the ultimate 'molecule of kindness', known as oxytocin. When we connect with someone, oxytocin flows through our brain and body. Its effects are multiple, including making us more trusting and more generous, helping keep our blood pressure low, healing our wounds and even preventing damage in the cardiovascular system.

The book also describes the impact of a loving, kind environment on the growth of an infant's brain. Comparisons of institutionalized children with children raised in stable homes show considerable differences in brain structure.

This is a book full of scientific studies, but it is certainly not an academic book. It is a broad-ranging one that is suitable for all, from teenagers to students, therapists, healthcare professionals, carers, doctors, nurses, politicians and even academics who wish to have a light read. And of course it is for the 'average' person too.

One of the most interesting points that it illustrates is that kindness is our nature. The human brain and nervous system have evolved over vast periods of time in an environment of close co-operative contact with others, where kind behaviour was necessary for survival. We are actually genetically wired to be kind. This is *why* it is good for us. And it is also why, when we don't show kindness, or compassion, gratitude or forgiveness, it stresses our nervous systems and is not so good for our health.

One form of kindness that is easy to miss is kindness towards ourselves. Few of us actually take good care of ourselves, and I hope the information presented here will encourage more people to do so.

At the end of the book there is a '21-Day Kindness Challenge' that you might want to try. There is also a section for schoolteachers that contains a number of ideas for helping children of all ages to develop kindness. And there is a list of 50 suggested acts of kindness to get you started.

I hope you enjoy the next few hundred pages. I have found it thoroughly rewarding writing them.

David R. Hamilton, PhD
September 2009

CHAPTER 1

KINDNESS IS THE BEST MEDICINE

'We cannot do great things on this earth, only small things with great love.'

Mother Teresa

In a 2000 study, 122 random people were given a flower. Everyone who received one responded positively, with women responding a little more positively than men. The authors of the study pointed out that in our modern fast-paced society people had learned to look out mostly for themselves and not so much for others. They wrote, 'This has become such a routine that we have forgotten to be kind to strangers for the sheer pleasure of helping a fellow human being.'[1]

It's nice to be kind and it's nice to be on the receiving end of an act of kindness. It makes everyone feel better.

And did you know that kindness is actually more attractive than good looks? That's the conclusion of a large study of 10,047 young people aged 20–25 from 33 different countries on six continents and five islands. Universally, without exception, in all cultures, when asked what they would most prefer in a mate, kindness was the number 1 quality. It trumped both good looks and financial prospects in women and men.[2]

Of course, it can be argued that appearance is initially what attracts people to each other, and that is true for many. But within a short time it's the person underneath that matters most of all. What we value most is what's in the heart.

Most of us even prefer friends who have a kind heart. In 'gossip studies', where psychologists listen in to participants talking about their friends and peers, the most common topics of conversation centre around kindness. Much of the gossiping is actually about those who don't show kindness.[3]

And not only is it attractive, but kindness is extremely good for our health, both physical and mental. In 2008 the 'Foresight Mental Capital and Wellbeing Project' was published by the UK Government Office for Science. Collecting data from a wide range of disciplines relating to mental health and collating them into a *Final Project Report*, it concluded that one of the '5 ways to mental wellbeing' was to 'Give.'

The highly prestigious report stated:

'Do something nice for a friend, or a stranger. Thank someone. Smile. Volunteer your time. Join a community group. Look out, as well as in. Seeing yourself, and your happiness, as linked to the wider community can be incredibly rewarding and creates connections with the people around you.'[4]

And not only is being kind good for our health, it also has an interesting side effect: it makes us happier.

IF YOU WANT TO BE HAPPY, BE KIND!

A 2008 study by scientists from the University of British Columbia in Canada showed that spending money on others was a sure-fire way to make yourself happier. The scientists asked 632 people to make a daily record of how they spent their money over the period of a month, noting everything from paying bills to shopping, eating lunch and giving donations to charities and gifts to others. They also had to rate their general level of happiness. The results showed that those who spent the most money on others were the happiest. Least happy were those who spent the least on others. The more we give, it seems, the happier we become.[5]

A 2004 study also showed that kindness produces happiness. Professor Sonja Lyubomirsky from the University of California had participants perform five random acts of kindness on a specific day once a week over a ten-week period. The results were clear: the acts of kindness made the participants happier.[6]

Another thing the study found was that it was important to vary the kind acts. Doing the same act several times didn't generate as many good feelings as doing a wide range of different acts. In fact, those people who did the same acts every day actually became less happy.

The study also found that making an effort was important. For instance, compare writing regular thank-you letters to writing one letter and sitting down with the person and reading it out to them. Which do you think would be the more powerful?

Kindness can even go beyond making us happy – it can make us *very* happy. This was shown in 2006 research published in the *Journal of Happiness Studies*. One study, involving 119 Japanese women (71 in the kindness group and 48 in the control group, for comparison), found that simply counting each act of kindness made them happier. The women were asked to take note for a whole week of when they were kind to others, keeping track of the number of kind acts each day and what they were. Using the Japanese Subjective Happiness Scale (JSHS), a scale that measures people's level of happiness, the women's levels of happiness were taken at the start and at the end of the study.

The simple act of counting kindnesses had a large impact on the participants' lives: they all became happier. But 20 of the participants didn't just become happier, they became *much* happier. It might be that this simple exercise of counting kindnesses can make around 70 per cent of the population happy and around 30 per cent of the population very happy.[7]

Many people get a high from doing good deeds for others. In regular charitable work it has even been called the 'helper's high'. In a large US study of the health, happiness and volunteering habits of 3,296 people, 95 per cent reported that they felt good when they helped someone. Fifty-four per cent said that they had an immediate warm feeling. Twenty-one per cent actually felt euphoric. And 29 per cent had more energy.

That was the 'helper's high', but the study went on to reveal that 57 per cent of the people had greater feelings of self-worth as a result and 53 per cent said that they felt happier and more optimistic. Eighty per cent reported that the feelings stayed with them for hours and sometimes even days afterwards. A summary of much of that research can be found in the excellent book *The Healing Power of Doing Good*, written by Allan Luks, the author of the study.[8]

In summarizing much of this study and some of his own personal observations, Luks also noted that helpers got fewer colds, less flu and fewer migraines, overate less and even slept better. Lupus sufferers who helped others reported less pain, and asthma sufferers had some relief from their symptoms. Patients who had had surgery even recovered more quickly when they helped others.

The effects of being kind are certainly broad-ranging and can lead to an overall improvement in mental, emotional and physical wellbeing. A 2001 study of 2,681 people conducted at Vanderbilt University, using data from the Americans' Changing Lives Survey, found that regular volunteering led to improvements in six aspects of wellbeing: happiness, life satisfaction, self-esteem, sense of control over life, physical health and lack of depression.[9]

And a 2008 study found that those who engaged in behaviour such as 'Volunteered my time', 'Gave money to a person in need' or 'Listened carefully to another's point of view' were happier, more satisfied with their lives and had a greater sense of wellbeing than those who 'Had sex purely to get pleasure', 'Bought a new piece of jewellery or electronics equipment just for myself' or even 'Went to a big party.'[10]

When we help another, or even simply give our time to someone, we become happier, healthier and more fulfilled.

HAPPINESS MAKES YOU RICHER

And when kindness brings us happiness, that happiness helps us make more money...

The happiness–income link was shown in a simple study of college students over a 16-year period. At the start of the study they were asked to rate their happiness level and 16 years later they were asked to do it again. The scientists then added together all that the students had earned over the entire period. They found that the happier they were at the start of the study, the more they earned throughout the 16-year period. In fact, those who had been happiest at the start of the study were earning, on average, $25,000 more per year at the end than those who had been least happy.[11]

Plenty of studies have shown that happiness leads not only to a higher income but also to more energy, better health, a longer lifespan, a more satisfying social life, more confidence and a higher quality of work.[12] Most people believe that these things are what make us happy, but most of the evidence suggests that it's the other way around. When we feel happy, these things come to us much more easily. Happiness, studies show, comes first.

So you want to be happier and enjoy all the benefits that it brings? Be kind. This was the sentiment of HH the Dalai Lama when he said, 'When we feel love and kindness towards others, it not only makes others feel loved and cared for, but it helps us also to develop inner happiness and peace.'

'GO OUT AND SERVE AND SEE YOUR DEPRESSION LIFT'

Kindness as a treatment for depression and other psychiatric disorders has been known for some time. 'Moral treatment' originated in Europe in the eighteenth century. In 1796, the English Quaker William Tuke founded the York Retreat, where 30 patients eventually lived as part of a small community. Receiving no medication or conventional therapeutic techniques, they were treated with kindness, compassion and respect (previous to this, many psychiatric patients had been tied up, flogged or locked away) and encouraged to build moral strength. A key component of their recovery was helping others.

The treatment spread to the USA, where it was the first established form of psychiatric care, becoming widespread in the

1820s and 1830s. It was practised up to 1875. Psychiatrists of the time believed that their methods led to 'organic changes in brain matter'.[13] It was a remarkable insight, because we know this to be true today.

In a large number of scientific studies, kindness has been found to alleviate depression in both the short and long term. An evening of helping out often works better than an antidepressant.

This was the experience of my friend Margaret McCathie. She suffered severe depression, making two suicide attempts and being kept in a locked ward for a month. She was given strong medication and several doses of electroconvulsive therapy, but nothing worked for her. One day, however, she sent a fax to Dr Patch Adams. Not expecting a response, she was surprised to receive a handwritten reply from Patch later that same day.

Margaret told me, 'Just feeling that he cared made all the difference.' In Patch's fax, which also described his own suicide attempts, he recommended, 'Go out and serve and see your depression lift.'

That is exactly what Margaret did. She made an effort to perform as many acts of kindness as she could. She did charitable work and helped people whenever she saw the opportunity. And, just as Patch Adams had said, her depression did indeed lift.

Margaret has never stopped being kind. In fact rarely have I come across an individual with so much kindness to give, and it's always completely selfless, with never the slightest hint of needing something in return. I often spend time with Margaret just to chat in the space of love and kindness and laughter (she is also a laughter therapist) that she creates.

Will Patch's advice work for everyone? Who knows? But if you are currently depressed, why not give it a try? What harm can it do? At the very least, you will be making a small difference to someone's life.

Several studies have shown the truth in Patch's wisdom. A 2003 University of Texas study, for instance, examined the mental health and volunteering habits of 3,617 adults over the age of 25. The results showed that there was a clear association between volunteering and reduced depression. Those who volunteered had fewer symptoms of depression than those who didn't. And the effect was found to be even stronger with adults over 65 years of age.[14]

A 2004 University of Wisconsin study found the same thing. Examining data on the volunteering habits and health of 373 people between the ages of 65 and 74, collected in the 1995 National Survey of Midlife Development in the USA, the researchers found that volunteering was protective against depression in older adults. Those who were volunteers reported less depression and more positive emotions than those who were not volunteers.[15]

Furthermore, a 2004 study of people over the age of 85 found a strong connection between altruism (selfless concern for the wellbeing of others) and happiness. Studying the responses of 366 people to statements like 'I place the needs of others ahead of my own', it found that those who were the most altruistic were the happiest and had the fewest symptoms of depression.[16]

Kindness in a volunteering capacity has also been shown to give older people a greater will to live. A 1981 study compared volunteers over 65 years of age to retired people of the same age group who didn't volunteer. Those who volunteered were found to be much more satisfied with their lives and to have fewer symptoms of depression, anxiety and somatization (which is where psychological states are expressed in the body as physical symptoms) and a stronger will to live than those who didn't volunteer.[17]

Nowadays, in New York State, many of the offices of mental health recommend that people with depression help others by getting involved in self-help groups.

THE BEST MEDICINE FOR KIDS AND TEENS

As well as being a symptom of depression, an inward focus on the self is a symptom of behavioural difficulties with some children. Kindness programmes, which encourage an outward focus on the happiness and wellbeing of others, have been shown to help such children.

For instance, in a US National Student Volunteer Program (NSVP), volunteering benefitted everyone, but difficult children got something more out of it: they became less self-centred and more focused on others than on themselves.

Back in 1973, black inner-city teenagers were asked to tutor fourth- and fifth-grade children with behavioural and personality problems for a study that was published in the *American Journal of Psychiatry*. When later evaluated, many of the teen tutors had improved in maths, reading and sentence completion tasks, and most of them showed positive changes in their attitude towards themselves, others, education and the future.[18]

In a US National Volunteer Service Program of the 1990s known as 'Teen Outreach', 695 high-school students were assigned to either a volunteer programme or a control group that didn't involve volunteering. The results were startling. In the group that volunteered there were considerably fewer teen pregnancies, much less failure at school and lower rates of academic suspension.[19]

In the UK, the city of London initiated a scheme in 2009 whereby teenage troublemakers who had had their Oyster travel cards taken from them as punishment could 'earn' them back by doing good deeds. In the first wave, at the time of writing, over 3,000 teenagers are being given the opportunity, over a period of four to eight weeks, to give something back to the community by volunteering. And when they do, their travel privileges will be returned.

RESISTANCE IS NOT FUTILE

Kindness is a key step in the AA 12-step programme. Recovering alcoholics help each other to get through difficult times and kindness plays an important part in their recovery.

A 2004 study conducted by scientists at Brown University Medical School examined the success rate of recovering alcoholics in abstaining from alcohol. The results showed that of those who helped other alcoholics, 40 per cent were able to avoid taking a drink in the following year. However, of those who didn't help other alcoholics, only 22 per cent were able to avoid having a drink. Helping other alcoholics is in fact the twelfth step in the famous AA 12-step programme. The offering of support to another not only increases the recovering addict's ability to resist the temptation of alcohol but also creates the inner feel-good factor that replaces cravings.

So compelling were the results of the study that the researchers recommended that: 'Clinicians who treat persons with substance abuse disorders should encourage their clients to help other recovering alcoholics to stay sober.'[20]

THE CHEMISTRY OF KINDNESS

On a chemical level, some evidence shows that kindness occupies the same neural circuits as addictive drugs. The helper's high comes in part from the release of endogenous opiates in the brain. Morphine and heroin are opiates, but endogenous opiates are those produced by the body – endogenous to the body. They provide a natural chemical substitute for alcohol or other drugs. So the only high experienced by successfully recovering addicts offering support to others is helper's high.

As well as opiates, serotonin and dopamine are released in the brain when we are kind. These help lift our mood and make us feel more positive and optimistic. In addition, when kindness involves an interaction between two people, a hormone called oxytocin is produced, which helps to strengthen bonds with others by making us feel more connected. So, whether kindness is alleviating depression or increasing happiness levels, chemicals are produced in the brain that contribute to establishing the new feelings on a chemical level.

In the longer term, practising kindness retrains neural pathways in the brain so that a formerly depressed person actually gets used to feeling good. The brain gets used to a certain level of opiates, serotonin, dopamine and oxytocin, just as a muscle gets used to a new flexibility after a person takes up gymnastics or yoga.

HOW KINDNESS CAN RELIEVE PAIN

Helping others is also a good antidote to pain. According to some people suffering recurring pain, it can be as good as pain-killing drugs. For some, plunging into performing acts of kindness is the only relief they get.

It is believed that the pain-relieving power of kindness comes in part from the endogenous opiates, also known as endorphins. Research shows that these bind to cells in the part of the brain involved in transmitting pain, taking the place of the chemicals that transmit pain signals and so interrupting the transmission of pain signals through the brain.

Some scientific studies have investigated the effects of kindness, in a volunteering capacity, on pain. One study, conducted in 2002 by nurses at Boston College in the USA, showed that patients suffering from chronic back pain benefitted greatly from helping other pain-sufferers. In what was described as a 'patient to peer' programme, the intensity of pain in the sufferers dropped significantly as a consequence of helping others. Depression and disability were also reduced.[21]

HELP WHEN YOU CAN ... BUT DON'T WEAR YOURSELF OUT

Several studies have shown that regular kindness is better for our health than no kindness at all or even just a little bit of kindness. Allan Luks' study showed this. He found that those who volunteered once a week had better mental and emotional health than those who volunteered once a year. In fact, of the health improvements noted in the study, there was a ten times greater chance that they were experienced by those who helped once a week than by those who helped once a year.[22]

A 2008 Australian National University study gathered some more precise information on how often we should help in a volunteer capacity if we want to fully enjoy the benefits of it. The researchers used data from the 'PATH Through Life' project, which was a population-based study of people aged 20–24, 40–44, 60–64 and 64–8. Using information from 2,126 adults aged 64–8, the researchers discovered that too much volunteering was almost the same as not volunteering at all. Health benefits were significant for those volunteering up to 100–200 hours a year (2–4 hours per week), but there was little difference in health benefits for more hours spent volunteering. However, for both men and women, health benefits began to decline beyond 800–1,000 hours a year (16–20 hours per week). The optimum health benefits for adults aged 64–8 came from volunteering between 2 and 16 hours a week.[23]

It seems that when volunteering becomes an obligation instead of something you feel drawn to do, it can take on the same feeling as a routine day job and the health benefits begin to fade.

One extra point to consider, though, is that this study involved people aged 64–8. I am not sure if the same pattern would be seen in all age groups. And individual differences in the meaning that people give to helping others matter. Two hours a week can have a very different effect on some than on others. This study and others like it represent an average over a large number of people, but they do bring a message that we should be aware of: help when you can, but don't wear yourself out.

Many carers, for example, don't get the same health benefits as occasional volunteers. Doctors who work too many hours are more likely to suffer from heart conditions than the average person. Many suffer from burnout. Many people give so much of themselves that the giving becomes an obligation. Then the mental and emotional benefits are erased.

A study involving 2,016 members of a church congregation found that those who regularly helped others had better mental health and lower rates of depression than those who helped on a less frequent basis. But, as they also found, 'giving beyond one's own resources is associated with worse reported mental health'.[24]

If you are a regular helper, find your own level where you can enjoy what you do without wearing yourself out. Then your kindness will go much further because your heart will be fully in it and you will reap the benefits of it too.

CONTAGIOUS KINDNESS

Another effect of kindness is that it is contagious. Being around kind people can make us kinder and healthier – as can just seeing them on TV. In a 1988 study by scientists at Harvard University, 132 students watched a 50-minute video of Mother Teresa performing acts of kindness. At the end of the video, the students had saliva swabs taken to measure levels of an important component of their immune systems known as salivary immuno-globulin-A (s-IgA), which is the body's first line of defence against pathogens in food. The levels had gone up, and when checked an hour later they were still elevated, which the scientists put down to the fact that the students 'continued to dwell on the loving relationships that characterized the film'.[25] In a nutshell, even just seeing acts of kindness can protect us from illness. This has been affectionately labelled the 'Mother Teresa effect'.

The contagious factor is especially important for children, as they naturally copy the behaviour of those around them. There has been much talk of the dangers of allowing children of a young age to watch violent movies, but what about the effects of children watching TV with a theme of kindness?

One study had children watching a video of some people bowling, but some of the children saw a different last part – they got to see the winner give his winning certificate to charity. When all of the children were later given certificates themselves, those who saw the donation part of the programme were more likely to give theirs away than the group who didn't see that part. The children were copying the kindness they had seen on TV.[26]

In another study, children watched a Lassie movie. Lassie's movies were very famous in the 1970s and millions of children around the world grew up learning of the stories of her courage and compassion. In the movie that the children watched for the study, some of them saw Lassie's owner rescue her puppies but some of them were not shown that piece. Afterwards, all the children played a game that was interrupted by the sounds of distressed puppies. Even though they would lose points in the game if they left, the children who had seen the puppies being rescued in the Lassie movie were more likely than the others to go to help.[27]

So, when we show kindness around children, it rubs off on them. If you want your children to have an attitude of kindness as they grow up, you can start today by leading by example.

KINDNESS MAKES THE HEART BEAT LONGER

Kindness also offers us some protection from the ageing process. A 1999 study of 1,972 community-dwelling residents in California conducted by the Buck Institute for Age Research, California, found that those who volunteered for two or more different organizations, who were labelled as 'high volunteers', had a 44 per cent lower mortality rate than those who didn't do any volunteering.[28]

A similar effect was found in a 2005 study of 7,527 community-dwelling people over 70 years of age. Following up after eight years, scientists from the Department of Veteran Affairs Health Care System and Stanford University discovered that frequent volunteers had a 33 per cent lower risk of mortality than people who didn't do any volunteering, and people who sometimes volunteered had a 25 per cent lower risk of mortality.[29]

Many religious or spiritual people have kindness as a central pillar of their beliefs. A 2002 University of Miami study showed that having spiritual and religious beliefs prolonged the lifespan of patients with HIV/AIDS. They found that a sense of peace, faith in God, religious behaviour and a compassionate view of others were all related to longer survival. Further analysis of the data revealed that altruistic behaviour, which including helping other HIV/AIDS sufferers, was also associated with longer survival.[30]

Altruism has also been shown to reduce levels of stress hormones in HIV patients, which may explain part of the longevity effects. Stress is one of the major factors that influence the rate of ageing and accelerate the course of disease. It is a curse of our time. In fact, the US Center for Disease Control and Prevention has estimated that around 90 per cent of all doctor visits in the USA are actually triggered by stress. It is a similar picture in most of the western world. The good news is that kindness is an antidote to stress and therefore buffers many of its physiologically damaging effects.

In 1976 Elizabeth Blackburn, PhD, one of *Time* magazine's '100 Most Influential People' in 2007, made the groundbreaking discovery of telomeres, which are the ends of DNA that prevent it from unravelling as cells divide. Telomeres thus protect the genetic information in the DNA, but recently it has been recognized that they also have an importance in ageing.

As we age, telomeres get shorter and thus cells have a limit to the number of times they can divide, which is known as the Hayflick limit. Many researchers believe that this puts a limit on what the human lifespan can be. On the other hand, other researchers believe that lengthening the telomeres or protecting them from shortening will make us live longer.

An analogy often used is to consider telomeres as the plastic ends of a pair of shoelaces. In time, through wear and tear, they shorten and the ends of the shoelaces begin to fray. In the same way, as we age, the telomere end caps on our DNA begin to wear and this means wear and tear on our body.

Mental and emotional stress is now known to speed up the rate of shortening of telomeres and cause faster ageing. Have you heard the stories of people who are under so much stress that their hair turns white almost overnight?

Attitude is known to powerfully impact the ageing process. In one study, optimists were shown to live around 7.5 years longer than pessimists.[31] Just as a positive attitude protects us from being ground down by the challenges of life, so it protects telomeres from being ground down and shortened.

As we learned previously, too much helping can wear us out and therefore become stressful, and this can also affect our telomeres. A piece of University of California at San Francisco research published in 2004 studied 39 healthy women who were the primary caregivers of a chronically ill child and 19 women of the same age who were mothers of healthy children. Each woman's stress level was measured using a standard stress questionnaire known to provide an accurate measure of psychological stress. Blood samples were taken from each of the women and the length of their telomeres measured.

In the 14 women with the highest stress scores, the average length of the telomeres was 3,110 units. In the 14 women who had the lowest stress scores, however, the average telomere length was 3,660 units. The most stressed women had telomeres that were 550 units shorter than those of the women who were least stressed. The authors of the study reported that the stressed women had lost telomere length equivalent to at least a decade of normal ageing.[32]

And it wasn't so much the stress itself that did the damage. We all have short-term periods of stress in our lives. This does not age us. The significant factor in the study was the number of years under stress. Those with the highest stress scores tended to be those who had been stressed the longest. It is long-term stress that ages us. So you needn't worry too much if you're under stress right now. It becomes a problem, though, if it continues for a while.

Similarly, in a 2007 study, scientists from the National Institute of Health and Ohio State University also found that the stress of caregiving shortened telomeres.[33] In the study, 41 caregivers of Alzheimer's patients were compared with non-caregivers. Blood samples were taken from each person and showed higher levels of stress chemicals in the blood of the caregivers. The caregivers who were experiencing chronic stress had significantly shorter telomeres. It was this chronic stress that caused the telomere-shortening.

In life, our attitude towards our circumstances and towards other people affects our stress levels and thus how fast or slowly we age. Viewing difficult situations as opportunities to be kind or compassionate can be a way around the telomere-shortening effects of the stress of long-term caregiving.

In the study of the caregivers of chronically ill children, the scientists pointed out that it was likely that the mothers with the longest telomeres were psychologically more resistant to the stresses in their lives. It is well known that stress-management techniques like meditation help us become more resistant to stressful situations. But viewing events differently, for example seeing something as an opportunity to be compassionate rather than as a difficulty, also helps us become more resistant. The change in perspective changes how we feel when facing a potentially stressful situation.

Of course, it's easier said than done. But knowing this can be a motivating factor to look at things in a different way. Whether we are caregivers or not, viewing 'difficult' people in our lives as a problem and getting annoyed with them does us little good. Seeing their behaviour as an opportunity for compassion, or to be kind, on the other hand, is life-enhancing for us in the present and may just add a few extra years onto our future.

TREATING EVERYONE AS EQUAL

Kindness involves treating people with equal respect, regardless of colour, creed or social status. This may have more importance than you might think. Studies show that everyday discrimination can lead to coronary artery calcification. A 2006 study of 181 middle-aged African-American women, for instance, found that those who felt discriminated against over a number of years, from many sources and not just racially, had higher levels of coronary artery calcification.[34]

Another study found a link between African-Americans who felt they suffered everyday discrimination and elevated diastolic blood pressure. The 2009 study involved 4,694 older adults, 60 per cent of whom were African-American and 60 per cent of whom were women, and found that the blood pressure effects of discrimination were felt by the African-Americans but not the whites.[35] It is likely that the psychological effects of discrimination run deeper for African-Americans than they do for whites.

LOVING-KINDNESS MEDITATION

An antidote to the stresses and strains of life, regardless of our problems, is meditation. A large number of studies have shown that it boosts the immune system, is good for the heart, reduces depressive symptoms, helps pain relief, slows ageing and improves overall mental and emotional wellbeing.

The Buddhist loving-kindness meditation (also known as *metta*) is a well-known meditation technique that leaves the meditator with warmth in their heart and, with practice, a feeling of love and affection towards everyone they know and have ever known.

The benefits are significant. A 2008 study conducted by psychologist Barbara Fredrickson of the University of North Carolina at Chapel Hill, involving 139 people, showed that a seven-week course of daily loving-kindness meditation increased participants' daily experiences of positive emotions, including love, joy, gratitude, contentment, hope, pride, interest, amusement and awe. This impacted them in many ways. They felt a greater sense of purpose and more mastery over their life. They even felt more optimistic. They also enjoyed improvements in the quality of their relationships and experienced better health. These positive benefits ultimately led to a greater sense of life satisfaction.[36]

Another benefit of the experiment was that positivity begat positivity. The increase in positive emotions felt after each week of meditation increased with practice. In the first week, using the well-known Likert scale, the increase in positive emotions was 0.06 units for each hour of meditation, but after seven weeks practice, one hour of meditation equated to 0.17 units increase in positive emotions.

Other research has found that the loving-kindness meditation is good for pain relief. In a 2005 study of a sample of people with chronic low back pain, an eight-week course of loving-kindness meditation significantly reduced pain, anxiety, anger and stress.[37] Other research has found that it helps build relationships too.[38]

Should you wish to try a loving-kindness meditation for yourself, here are some instructions:

HOW TO DO A LOVING-KINDNESS MEDITATION

Start by sitting or lying comfortably. Relax and pay attention to your breathing, breathing in a slow, comfortable rhythm.

Now bring your attention to your heart and say, either out loud or mentally, 'May I be well. May I be happy. May I be at ease.'

Now think of someone you love or care about. This time say, either out loud or mentally, 'May you be well. May you be happy. May you be at ease.'

Do this for all of your loved ones. You can name them individually if you like by inserting their name in place of 'you'.

Now move on to other people in your life – friends, work colleagues, people whom you see from time to time – and repeat the same process, inserting their name.

Then move on to people you don't get on with.

Keep this going in an ever-widening circle until you wish wellbeing, happiness and ease for the whole world, including people you consider to be enemies.

You don't have to do all the circles in one go. A shortened version is just to wish wellbeing, happiness and ease for your loved ones. You can take the circle as wide as you wish.

AN EXTRA NOTE ON KINDNESS

I have included several studies of people volunteering in this chapter, but there is a lot of kindness we can show in our daily lives that does not involve volunteering. We don't need to wait around for a two-hour slice of structured time.

Kindness is a way, not a thing. And as we show kindness in our lives, the way becomes even clearer. Negative behaviour fades away as it is replaced by the warm feeling that kindness brings. As Albert Schweitzer wrote, 'Constant kindness can accomplish much. As the sun makes ice melt, kindness causes misunderstanding, mistrust, and hostility to evaporate.'

They do evaporate and it is their destiny to do so in all of our lives, because, as we will see later, it is our nature to be kind. When we don't take up the opportunities to be kind that the world presents to us every day, we betray that nature. The multiple benefits are then lost as opportunities slip away. But when we are kind, we make everyone's life just that little bit better.

STORIES OF KINDNESS

One Good Turn Deserves Another

My sister was shopping in Los Angeles with my 81-year-old mother. My mom fell outside one of the stores and hurt her wrist. Fortunately there was a trauma nurse in the parking lot and he came over and kindly bandaged her up. He was extremely nice and caring towards her. The store manager also came out with ice for her wrist. She received so much kindness.

A few days later, my sister was going out for a meal. When she entered the restaurant, who was there but the nurse who had tended my mom's wrist, together with his wife. My sister quietly paid for their meal without them knowing.

It's amazing that she bumped into the nurse. Los Angeles is not exactly a small place. **Ileen**

A Friend Indeed

I was due to go to a party and was so looking forward to it. I don't exactly get out that much, as I am a single mum. But then I got a call from my babysitter: she wasn't well and couldn't come. A friend who had arranged to pick me up then knocked on my door, all dressed up to the nines, only to meet an exasperated and under-dressed woman with two kids on her hands.

I told her just to go on and enjoy herself, but she was having none of it. She flew into action and called up every babysitter that I had ever used. She found one that was free and then told me to get dressed – quickly! – and got the kids ready to go in her car. Moments later, we were on our way to the babysitter's.

We dropped the kids off and arrived at the restaurant where all our colleagues were – just an hour late.

My point is, my friend could easily have left me at the house and got to the dinner on time, but she didn't. My happiness was important to her and she sacrificed some of her evening for me: kindness to a tee. **Carolyn**

CHAPTER 2

'I FEEL FOR YOU': THE POWER OF COMPASSION

'Compassion is not religious business, it is human business. It is not luxury, it is essential for our own peace and mental stability, it is essential for human survival.'

HH The Dalai Lama

There was a Tibetan monk who was held prisoner for over 20 years in a Chinese gulag. There he was banned from practising his traditions, placed in solitary confinement and even tortured. After his release, HH the Dalai Lama asked him what his biggest stress was. It turned out not to be the physical pain or isolation, as one would expect. He said that it was his fear that he would lose compassion for his jailers.

His compassion came through practising compassion. We, too, have the potential to develop huge amounts of compassion. You might ask why we would want this. Well, compassion is very good for your health, as you will see from the remainder of this chapter. But it's also good for everyone else. It can make the world a better place. Many of our ethics are founded on compassion, and ethics govern how we interact with each other. Peace and harmony in our world depend on compassion – they depend on our capacity to see through the eyes of other people. Also, when we see others suffering and feel compassion for them, we are motivated to act with kindness.

Compassion can change us so profoundly that it is all we exude. When talking about love, Dr Wayne W. Dyer once drew the analogy with squeezing an orange. He said, 'Squeeze an orange and out comes orange juice, because that's all that's inside.' Similarly, then, if we develop enough compassion, when we're squeezed, which might be when we're stressed, hurt or offended, all that will come out of us is compassion, because that's all we'll have inside. We'll look not at our pains and challenges, but at those who are causing us pain, and we'll begin to understand their pain, the pain that is driving them, and feel compassion for them. Then we'll be free.

This may not sound that easy, but compassion can be developed. MRI studies now show that thinking the same kinds of thoughts over and over again – in this case it would be thoughts about compassion – causes structural changes in the brain. Millions of connections are born between cells in the relevant area of the brain, which actually increases the depth and size of that area. MRI studies of the brains of Tibetan monks show substantial activation of the left frontal lobes, an area associated with compassion. That area is also considerably larger in Tibetan monks than in normal people. In fact, when psychologists first studied Tibetan Buddhists, they thought there was a fault with their instruments. The power readings from the monks' brains were so high that they were unlike anything that had been seen before. Years of meditation and compassion training had significantly impacted their brains.

It doesn't take years for the changes to take place, though. In fact, one study showed that when non-meditators were taught to meditate for just six weeks, there was a proliferation of growth and activity in their left frontal lobes too as compassion took root in their nervous systems.[1]

EMPATHY: 'I FEEL *WITH* YOU'

Compassion grows out of empathy. Empathy has been called 'feeling with'. It is where we share another's pain. Compassion, on the other hand, is 'feeling *for*'. We acknowledge the pain and have a compassionate desire for the person to be free of it. Therefore empathy is where caring for others begins. Cultivating empathy makes acting with compassion and kindness much more likely. Wouldn't that be a powerful pathway of change in our lives, and in the world?

I was inspired by Barack Obama's remarks on empathy in a speech he made on 11 August 2006, before he became president. He said:

'You know, there's a lot of talk in this country about the federal deficit. But I think we should talk more about our empathy deficit – the ability to put ourselves in someone else's shoes; to see the world through the eyes of those who are different from us – the child who's hungry, the steelworker who's been laid-off, the family who lost the entire life they built together when the storm came to town. When you think like this – when you choose to broaden your ambit of concern and empathize with the plight of others, whether they are close friends or distant strangers – it becomes harder not to act; harder not to help.'

This is why empathy is quite often where kindness begins. We share another's pain, then compassion arises as we wish them free of suffering, and then we are motivated to help with an act of kindness.

The interesting thing is that we are wired for empathy. The brain's 'empathy circuit' lights up when we see a person in pain. In a sense, the brain can't distinguish between whether they are suffering or we are suffering. When we see someone suffering, our brain reproduces the same emotions in us.

It's similar to the way our brain mirrors the motions and facial expressions of those around us. We know that seeing someone move their hand, for instance, activates 'mirror neurons' in a region of the brain known as the pre-motor cortex and this activates the actual neurons involved in hand moving (the motor cortex). This, in turn, stimulates the muscles in the hand. Seeing someone move their hand, then, stimulates our own hand.

As odd as this might sound, it is currently being trialled as a pioneering new therapy for the rehabilitation of stroke patients, and early results have been very positive. Stroke patients benefit from observing the movements of able-bodied people, something known as 'action observation', because their muscles are stimulated as if they are really moving.[2] (For interest, I discussed some of these studies in my book *How Your Mind Can Heal Your Body*.)

In a similar way, the 'empathy circuit' of the brain mirrors the emotional state of those around us. When we see someone in pain, our empathy circuit kicks into gear and causes us to share some of their pain.

The other side of it is that if we see someone who is happy, our brain produces a happy state in us. This is why a happy person can walk in through the door and change the mood of an entire room. We notice their body language and our mirror neurons kick in, altering our own body language, and we pick up on their emotions, partly through their eyes and facial expressions, and our empathy circuit kicks in, reproducing the same emotions in us.

Tania Singer, one of the leaders in the field of the neuroscience of empathy, writes, 'Consistent evidence shows that sharing the emotions of others is associated with activation in neural structures that are also active during first-hand experience of that emotion.'[3]

This even happens when we see someone in physical pain. We don't actually feel the physical pain, although our mirror neurons can give us a twinge, but we feel the subjective, or emotional, part of it. Our brain is activated in much the same way as theirs, just minus the sensory bit where the painful sensation is processed. Everything else is the same.[4]

This was shown in a 2004 experiment where 16 couples were either given a painful electric shock to their hand or watched it happening to their partner. Specifically, in one part of the experiment the woman's brain was scanned while a painful stimulus was applied to her hand. In another part, her brain was scanned again, not while she received the pain but while she watched her partner's hand receiving the pain. The activity of her brain in both situations was almost identical. The only parts that weren't activated when she watched her partner's pain were those involved in the actual physical sensation of the pain. The emotional components were identically activated in both cases. On an emotional level, she felt the way she felt her partner felt. She was empathizing.[5]

The degree of brain activation is proportional to our reading of the pain intensity. If we imagine the pain to be great, the brain is greatly activated and we feel strong empathy. If we imagine the pain to be minor, the activation and empathy are also minor. A

2006 study showed this. There was substantial brain activation when a needle deeply penetrated a person's hand, but not when they received only a pinprick.[6]

There is some evidence that we detect the intensity of another person's pain from their face, as our mirror neurons and empathy neurons systems pick up minute changes in facial expression that signify pain.[7]

As an aside, the potential exists for us to feel the physical pain as well. In a 2007 study, when a needle pierced a person's hand, for instance, an onlooker's primary somatosensory cortex, which is the region of the brain *directly* connected to the sense of the hand and responsible for the sense of touch, was activated.[8]

But it's not just the brain that's activated when we see others suffering. We all know how it feels when we see heart-wrenching images of starving children – we feel a lump in our throat and our heart rate and breathing change. Nerves from the brain stimulate a physical-emotional response too. So the brain mirrors the emotional states of the people around us and makes us feel the physical effects of them.[9]

Empathy is completely natural to us. It takes work to block it. We sometimes have to convince ourselves that people are bad or are out to take advantage of our good nature in order not to feel it. As Diane Berke, an interfaith minister and a leading figure in interfaith ministry education, said, 'The major block to compassion is the judgement in our minds. Judgement is the mind's primary tool of separation.'[10]

EMPATHY AND COMPASSION

As we have seen, compassion grows out of empathy. There is actually a similarity in brain activation between empathy and compassion. The main difference with compassion is the additional activation of the prefrontal cortex, as empathy moves to a more conscious experience and we know we want the suffering to end.

Some recent research by scientists at the University of Wisconsin has illustrated the neural similarity between empathy and compassion.[11] The scientists showed that cultivating compassion indeed impacted the neural circuits involved in empathy. Also active in compassion was the prefrontal cortex, allowing us to make a choice to care. They also found that compassion had a stronger effect than empathy. Generation of compassion actually enhanced the neural circuits involved in empathy. It turned them up, so to speak.

The scientists compared the brains of expert meditators trained in the regular practice of a compassion meditation to those of novice meditators who were unfamiliar with the meditation. They also compared the brains of the experts and novices when positive sounds (like a laughing baby), negative sounds (like someone distressed) and neutral ones were played. In each case, the neural responses of the experts were much higher.

Much of the experts' practice had been in a loving-kindness-compassion meditation that produced, as the scientists wrote, 'an unconditional readiness and availability to help living beings'. For the study, the novices were taught it and scans were taken of their brains while they performed it. Compared with the novices', the experts' brains were much more activated when the sounds were played. Their empathy muscle was stretched, so to speak.

The study showed that compassion could not only be learned but also that it exercises the brain, in much the same way that a muscle's range increases the more we flex it. Practising compassion every day flexes the areas of the brain that process it, not only making it easier to feel compassion in the future but also impacting the fine structure of those brain areas. And just as a muscle grows through being worked, so the compassion area of the brain grows through the practice of compassion. Neuro-scientists often draw this comparison between the brain and a muscle.

The scientists in the study also pointed out that the increased activation in one part of the brain (insula) was consistent with a larger thickness of the cortex there, demonstrating significant neural growth in that area. The insula part of the empathy circuit had grown due to compassion practice. Compassion actually changes the brain. No longer can it be thought of as all in the mind – it causes measurable structural changes in the brain.

Practising a loving-kindness-compassion type of meditation on a daily basis not only changes the brain but also seems to enhance the seemingly natural tendency to wish everyone well and think the best of people. As a result, when situations arise that challenge us, positive feelings towards others arise much more easily than before. Instead of becoming stuck in feelings of irritation, judgement, frustration, even blame or hurt, which accompany the average person for most of the day after they have been offended, compassion takes over and peace sets in. We spontaneously recognize that the person who has hurt us could themselves be in pain and that it could be causing them to behave in that way.

This spontaneous recognition of another's pain is natural, but it is normal for many of us to overrule it with personal judgements about people. Compassion practice helps us to put the judge-ments aside and, in a sense, return to our natural state. Can you imagine the emotional freedom in not having to suffer, complain or run annoyances over and over in your head all day long?

I've spoken a lot about sharing another's pain, but it's not just pain that stimulates us to share the feelings of others. As already mentioned, we also feel joy when others feel joy. In a nutshell, compassion practice helps you feel happy when others are happy and feel empathy and love when they are sad, and it frees you from internal suffering and puts you back in touch with who you really are. And you wondered why some Buddhist monks smile a lot!

HOW TO DO A LOVING-KINDNESS-COMPASSION MEDITATION

Sit comfortably and quietly and spend a moment or two focusing on your breathing. Take slow, regular breaths.

Now think of someone you care about and genuinely wish them wellbeing and freedom from pain and suffering. You can use the words, 'May you be well. May you be happy. May you be free from suffering,' if you find that easier, but the words are not as important as the sentiment.

Do this for a few different people whom you care about.

Oh, and don't forget to start with yourself!

In time, you can extend your meditation to people you interact with, like work colleagues.

And with practice, you can extend it to your enemies, or people who have hurt you, and eventually wish the entire world freedom from suffering.

COMPASSION BENEFITS THE IMMUNE SYSTEM

Eric Hoffer, the noted writer and philosopher, wrote, 'Compassion is the antitoxin of the soul: where there is compassion even the most poisonous impulses remain relatively harmless.'

There is actually strong evidence that compassion directly benefits our physical health. A 2009 study involving 61 people aged between 17 and 19 examined the impact of a compassion meditation on interleukin-6 and cortisol levels when a person was stressed. Interleukin-6 is a substance known as a pro-inflammatory cytokine and is involved in inflammation. Too much in the body can be a signal of disease. It is also well known that stress impacts disease. Chronic stress, in fact, over a long period of time, makes disease more likely. It has been associated with heart problems, cancer, arthritis, diabetes, dementia, major depression and much more.

Scientists monitor the impact of stress on the body by measuring levels of specific chemicals in the blood or saliva. Under stress, for instance, cortisol, which is classically referred to as a stress hormone, increases. Levels of interleukin-6 also rise, and this causes inflammation in the body, which is known to have a hand in the creation of a number of diseases. Recent research now suggests that cortisol may encourage increases in interleukin-6 and together they may impact disease development by suppressing the immune system.

In the study, 33 people were given six weeks training in a compassion meditation and the other 28 were in a control group, so didn't do any meditation. Then both groups were given a task in the lab that was designed to stress them. The results showed that compassion meditation training significantly reduced levels of interleukin-6. Compared with those who didn't meditate, the meditators had levels that were much lower. They also reported less psychological stress. Overall, their stress levels were more than 50 per cent lower than those of the non-meditators.

The key with the compassion meditation was that it took practice. The participants who attended the most meditation classes and did the most practice had the greatest reductions in interleukin-6 and the least stress. Those who only practised a little (one or two meditation sessions per week) had interleukin-6 levels that were very similar to those in the control group. But as the number of sessions per week increased, the levels of interleukin-6 came down a lot, with those who undertook six or more sessions per week enjoying the greatest benefits.[12]

When events in life leave us stressed, cortisol and interleukin-6 usually increase, especially if the situations are long-lasting and we can't shake off the stress. But compassion meditation buffers the effects of stressful life situations, not only psychologically by making us feel better, but also physically by reducing the actual biological agents of potential illness in our bodies, thereby protecting us from illness.

There are few medications that can reduce interleukin-6 levels in the body without undesirable side effects. Yet compassion does it for us. Putting this into perspective, when we share the suffering of another person and wish them free of that suffering, our own health improves.

As a regular meditator since 2000, I can honestly say that I have noticed the benefits of accumulated time spent meditating. When I have periods when I don't meditate regularly, when I convince myself that there are more important things to do with a 20-minute period of time in a whole day of 24 hours, the benefits of a calm mind gradually leave me and are gradually replaced with feelings of stress as I juggle the workload in my life.

STORIES OF KINDNESS

A Change of Heart

I was in my car going to collect my elderly friend Dorothy. On the way I reached the bottom of a large and steep hill and saw a guy struggling up it carrying a large TV.

I stopped and offered him a lift. He was extremely grateful to me. We both lifted the TV into the car and I drove him up and over the hill to the other side. We took the TV out of the car and he offered me some money for helping him. I think he might have thought I was a taxi driver.

I refused, but he was insistent. So I made a deal with him. I said, 'Instead of giving me money, do something kind for someone.' He thought this was a good idea. We said our goodbyes and I drove on to collect Dorothy.

We were driving back about 10 minutes later when we saw the man carrying the TV back up the hill again.

I pulled up alongside him and asked him what he was doing. He said, 'I'm taking the damn thing back!'

He had stolen the TV. **Tom**

A Welcome Call

Around 20 years ago when I was having a particularly stressful time and was deeply unhappy and lonely, my phone rang one lunchtime with a song playing over the line. That song was Stevie Wonder's I Just Called to Say I Love You. *I never did discover who the caller was (no caller ID in those days), but it certainly helped my state of mind at the time.* **Mary**

CHAPTER 3

HAVING THE NERVE TO BE COMPASSIONATE

'The dew of compassion is a tear.'

Lord Byron

There is actually a nerve known as the nerve of compassion in the body. This is the vagus nerve. Vagus means 'wandering', from the Latin, and the nerve gets its name from the way it wanders around the body. It is in fact the longest nerve in the body. Starting from the brainstem, it meanders through the face and thorax and then down through the major organs of the body, including the heart, lungs, kidneys, liver, stomach, intestines, colon and spleen.

As you might imagine, this nerve plays an important role in the body. It influences the coordinated muscle contractions in the stomach that are required to digest food and also serves as a natural brake on heart rate, keeping it relatively low. Without the work of the vagus nerve, the average person's heart rate would be around 115 bpm. When we breathe out, the vagus nerve is working and reduces heart rate. When we breathe in, we let the vagus 'brake' off a little and heart rate speeds up. Breathing out again applies the vagus brake and heart rate once again slows down. This moment-to-moment variation in heartbeat is called heart rate variability, and measuring it can give us some information on vagus nerve activity, or vagal tone, as it is often called.

Studies show that high vagus nerve activity, or vagal tone, translates to high compassion and vice versa.

FEELING CLOSER

Just as a doctor, nurse or carer is drawn to people they can help, so compassion draws us to people who are suffering or vulnerable. Indeed, studies now show that people who are more compassionate tend to feel more of a sense of kin with weak or vulnerable people than with strong people.

In a 2009 University of California at Berkeley study, for instance, 202 participants were shown a list of 19 different groups, some of which were 'strong' groups, like professional athletes, politicians and celebrities, and some 'weak' groups, like orphans, homeless people or the elderly. The participants were then asked which group they felt they were most like. The study found that high vagus nerve activity translated to a greater feeling of closeness to the weaker and more vulnerable groups. Those with high vagal tone felt themselves to be most like the weak groups.[1]

A QUESTION OF POWER

We all have a perception of the power of individuals and groups. In psychology research, this power refers to the influence that a person exerts over other people's outcomes in life. 'High-power' individuals are those who seem to have control over some of the lives of 'low-power' individuals. For instance, a typical CEO would be labelled a high-power individual whereas a typical blue-collar worker would be labelled a low-power individual.

Studies actually show that low-power individuals tend to be more compassionate than high-power individuals.[2] This is not meant as a negative reflection on high-power people, only an indication that the roles they tend to play in life generally desensitize them to the emotions of other people. For instance, many have to make financial or organizational decisions that impact the lives of low-power people, sometimes in a way that is not beneficial to those people. In time, it becomes easier to not think about the consequences to the low-power people – that they may lose their homes, or that their children may go hungry. With less activity in the high-power person's brain empathy circuits, compassion is turned down. The compassion muscle isn't being exercised, so to speak, so it weakens.

Low-power individuals, on the other hand, generally experience less sense of control over their lives than high-power individuals do and less freedom to do as they wish. They also experience more of the negative consequences of decisions they have not made and thus experience harder times in a general sense. As they tend to form relationships with other low-power individuals, they become more acutely aware of the challenges and pains of each other's lives than high-power individuals do. A typical conversation between high-power individuals might centre around opportunities or future plans, but a typical conversation between low-power individuals might focus on how to cope with difficulties that they feel they have little control over. And this is a breeding ground for compassion.

However, although the compassion muscles of low-power individuals generally have more regular workouts than those of high-power individuals and are thus stronger, high-power individuals can train in compassion. And the more that compassion floods their conscious nature, the more they move their attention away from results and outcomes and towards people and how they feel.

Of course, these power studies reflect a broad generalization because we all know many exceptions to the rule. The Pope, the Dalai Lama, Nelson Mandela and Gandhi, for instance, are popular figures that fall into the high-power category but have shown extraordinary amounts of compassion. And even if a work environment doesn't lend itself to compassion, many high-power individuals have personal circumstances that do breed compassion. I'm sure, in fact, that each of us personally knows a number of high-power individuals who are warm and compassionate people.

It is also my personal belief that the more compassionate (or what we might even consider 'softer') people take the reins in industry, business and government, the better for all of us. This will foster more peace and more sharing between businesses and between nations, as leaders consider more the impact of their decisions upon the lives of others.

The growth opportunities for high-power individuals are in cultivating compassion and walking in two worlds – being able to make high-power decisions while at the same time considering the impact of these decisions on others in a sympathetic way. History is more likely to remember the names of people like this.

Compassion is not weakness, as many believe. It is a mark of great strength.

WE TRUST IN COMPASSION

And if you are a compassionate person, people will trust you more.

How do we know this? Facial expressions and body language often give us more accurate clues to people's real feelings and motivations than what they say or how they act. Even tiny momentary flashes of emotion on a person's face can be 'seen' by our nervous systems. They detect facial expressions even when we're not consciously paying attention to them or when they occur so fast that we can't consciously register them. For example, studies show that photos of sad faces shown ultra-fast activate the amygdala in the brain, the region that processes fear and anxiety.[3]

You may have had the type of experience where someone pretending to be nice has displayed a millisecond of anxiety while trying to sell you something, for instance. That is a signal that they may not be telling the truth or fully believe what they are saying. And although you don't consciously register it, your brain still picks it up. The result is that you get an odd feeling about the person. You're not sure they're trustworthy.

Some researchers in the field of emotional research have mastered a technique known as the facial action coding system (FACS), developed by the psychologist Paul Ekman, in which they break down videos of people and study them frame by frame so that they can identify the range of emotions that only appear for tiny fractions of a second on their face. Studies in this area clearly show that our facial expressions, even in very brief flashes, tell another person's nervous system what's really going on in our heart or mind.

In a University of California at Berkeley study, two participants played a game that involved making financial decisions that affected each other. Afterwards, other participants watched videos of the game but the sound was muted so that they couldn't hear what the players were saying to each other, only see their body language and the expressions on their faces.

When they finished watching the videos, they had to say which of the two players they felt was more trustworthy. It turned out that the players who were considered most trustworthy were the ones with the highest vagal tone. In other words, the participants trusted the compassionate players more.[4]

So the more compassionate you are, the more likely people are to trust you. If you want to succeed, this might be quite useful in both your business life and your personal life.

COMPASSION IN KIDS

High vagal tone equates with compassion in children too. Studies have shown that 7/8-year-old children with high resting vagal tone are more helpful in class and show more compassion than children with low vagal tone.[5]

In another study, a group of children watched videotapes of children who had been injured in accidents and were now in hospital. All of the group had their vagal tone measured and those who had the highest tones were the ones who were most likely to volunteer to take homework to the injured children in hospital.[6]

VAGAL TONE AND GETTING THROUGH LIFE

Adult studies have shown that having a high vagal tone also helps us cope with the stresses and strains of daily life. It's probably because of the way the vagus nerve helps us relax by controlling heart rate and helping reduce blood pressure. People with high vagal tone who suffer the loss of a partner, for instance, recover from the depression associated with their grief more quickly.

In a 2005 study, 35 bereaved participants wrote about their bereavement and how they felt about their former partner and about events from the past. Those with the highest vagal tone benefitted most from the exercise.[7]

Studies also show that university students with high vagal tone handle the stresses of university life better.[8]

It is no surprise that many people suffering from severe depression show very low vagal tone. Their nervous system is not set to 'rest and relax'. And in a state of depression, we are much more focused on our personal pain than on other people and find it more difficult to show compassion to others.

A new treatment for depression, which has seen very powerful results in treatment-resistant depression of severely depressed people, is vagus nerve stimulation. In fact, so good is it that the US FDA approved it for use in 2009 for this category of depression. Studies show that not only does it stimulate the vagus nerve but that it might also initiate neurogenesis (growth of brain cells) in the hippocampus of the brain, which is what some powerful antidepressants are believed to do.

People who are less severely depressed might benefit from natural vagus nerve stimulation. Training in compassion might help, or being placed in volunteer environments where their capacity for sympathy will naturally develop. And from there, the desire to be kind might develop too, which would lead to a greater sense of inner happiness. This might not be the remedy for everyone, but it might be the ideal roadmap for many people with mild to moderate depression.

THE INFLAMMATORY REFLEX

Taking a look at another of the capacities of the nerve of compassion, when we have an injury or infection, chemicals known as cytokines make their way to the injured or infected site. There are two kinds of cytokines: those that promote inflammation are known as *pro*-inflammatory cytokines and those that reduce inflammation are known as *anti*-inflammatory cytokines. When the pro-inflammatory cytokines reach the site of injury or infection, they cause inflammation, which is an important part of the healing process and results in redness and swelling. However, if the infection is severe, some of these cytokines can spill out into the bloodstream and this causes collateral damage, poisoning our blood and organs. There is a delicate balance between pro-inflammatory cytokines and anti-inflammatory cytokines that generally helps to prevent this. But there is a danger that anti-inflammatory cytokines too can spill out into the bloodstream, and they suppress the immune system, which can lead to the possibility of other infections or illnesses.

Recent research has shown, however, that the body has a much more efficient method of preventing the overproduction and spillage of pro-inflammatory cytokines, and this involves the vagus nerve. As well as working as a natural brake on heart rate, it also serves as a natural brake on the production of pro-inflammatory cytokines. The vagus nerve endings, which touch every organ in the body, sense where the injury is and then prevent the overproduction of pro-inflammatory cytokines at that site.

A discovery of massive importance, made in 2000 by Kevin J. Tracey, this is now known as the 'inflammatory reflex'. Tracey writes, 'The nervous system reflexively regulates the inflammatory response in real time [via the vagus nerve], just as it controls heart rate and other vital functions.'[9] Such is the importance of this discovery to medicine that a Nobel conference dedicated to it was organized at the Karolinska Institute in Stockholm in September 2004.

Specifically, the vagus nerve endings release a chemical known as acetylcholine, which sticks like glue to regions known as receptors on the surface of some immune cells. This sends a signal to the DNA inside the cells that tells it to stop making some pro-inflammatory cytokines (specifically, one known as tumour necrosis factor, TNF). By this process, the vagus nerve serves as a protection against sepsis (poisoning caused by infection).

Several studies have indeed now shown that stimulating the vagus nerve can prevent multiple organ damage caused by severe infection and, amazingly, where there is already multiple organ damage, some of it can be reversed.[10]

TURNING THE TAP OFF

When the cytokine 'tap' is working properly and cytokines flow through the body when required, they successfully help eradicate invading pathogens and prevent sepsis. But sometimes the tap doesn't go fully off, but drips. This can be a consequence of prolonged mental and emotional stress, or even arise though poor diet or other unhealthy lifestyle choices. But the problem is that the drip can lead to a gradual build-up of internal inflammation throughout the body.

Think of it like this: with a dripping tap at home, water might eventually spill out onto the floor and cause damage. In the same way, a dripping cytokine tap in the body can spill pro-inflammatory cytokines around the body, causing collateral damage in the heart, blood vessels, brain, other organs – in fact, pretty much everywhere. Indeed, excess pro-inflammatory cytokines can lead to a number of medical conditions, including cancer, heart disease, inflammatory bowel disease, atherosclerosis, hay fever, autoimmune conditions like rheumatoid arthritis, lupus, multiple sclerosis, diabetes and myasthenia gravis, transplant rejection, fragility and frailty, and can accelerate the ageing process. New research has even found a link between inflammation and Alzheimer's. In fact, Russell Tracy, who is a professor of pathology and biochemistry at the University of Vermont College of Medicine, said, 'Inflammatory factors predict virtually all bad outcomes in humans.'[11]

Compassion, then, by training the vagus nerve and effectively turning off the tap, might just be much better for us than we ever imagined. It's probably one of the reasons why meditation, specifically compassion meditation, reduces levels of the pro-inflammatory cytokine interleukin-6, as we learned in the last chapter. Our natural activation of the vagus nerve through long-term practice of compassion might offer many of us some form of general protection from disease. Although not an instant fix, it might just keep the tap from dripping.

Research may soon find that stimulating the vagus nerve could treat Alzheimer's and halt the progression of cancer, heart disease and many other conditions. We may even discover that activating the vagus nerve as a daily practice, through reducing stress and increasing kindness and compassion, could offer us background protection from these conditions. Of course, this is purely conjecture, as the research hasn't been done yet, but I will hazard an educated guess that this is what we will find.

THE VAGUS NERVE AND AGEING

The conventional view is that ageing is just something that happens with the passage of time, but gerontologists have now suggested that it is in fact caused by inflammation, or that inflammation is at least one of the main factors that cause it. Certainly, inflammation increases as we age, and many gerontologists now suggest that one of the keys to longevity is to treat inflammation as we would any other condition. There's even talk of finding a 'wonder drug', a type of anti-inflammatory drug that could also be used to treat diabetes, atherosclerosis, some cancers and even Alzheimer's. But evidence is now emerging that the wonder drug is not so much a drug but a nerve – the vagus nerve. Some evidence is indeed suggesting that it impacts some of the 'major agers': telomere shortening, inefficiency of mitochondria and low nitric oxide levels.

In the first chapter we looked at shortening telomeres and their ageing effect. It is believed that persistent inflammation in the body can speed up their shortening, grinding them down, so to speak. And since high vagal tone is associated with low inflammation, it has been suggested that the vagus nerve might actually slow the ageing process by increasing the lifespan of telomeres.[12] Thus, compassion helps us live longer.

Another of the major agers is having inefficient mitochondria. Mitochondria are the power units of cells and turn food into energy. But in the process of this they also produce free radicals. As we age, they become less efficient and some of the free radicals can spill out into the body, which can increase susceptibility to a number of diseases, including heart disease and ageing. Free radicals are in fact known to accelerate telomere shortening. Inflammation also creates free radicals and some of these can damage mitochondria. Thus the vagus nerve can impact mitochondrial health and efficiency by reducing free radicals throughout the body.

Another major ager is not having enough nitric oxide. This plays a key role in dilating blood vessels, lowering blood pressure and keeping the heart healthy. Our ability to generate nitric oxide reduces as we age. It has now been shown that activation of the vagus nerve produces nitric oxide, or stimulates it into action, thus relaxing and dilating blood vessels and lowering blood pressure. Indeed, in a groundbreaking 2009 study performed by scientists from the University of Leicester and the University of

Birmingham in the UK, stimulating the vagus nerve was shown to increase levels of nitric oxide in the heart.[13]

A simple and natural way to increase nitric oxide levels is to breathe deeply through the nose, as we do in meditation. This also activates the vagus nerve and thus serves as an efficient way to slow down ageing and prevent some damage to the heart. And since we breathe deeply in meditation, it explains why meditation has been shown in so many studies to be good for the heart.[14]

So, if we want to slow our rate of ageing, we would do well to increase our vagal tone. And one of the simplest ways of doing this is through practising compassion whenever the opportunity arises to share the pain of another and ease their suffering.

SPICING UP THE VAGUS NERVE

In time, just as a muscle becomes more toned through exercise, so the vagus nerve will become more toned as we exercise our capacity for compassion. Practising compassion may, in time, stop the drip of pro-inflammatory cytokines into the body.

Some studies have shown that meditation and hypnosis can reduce inflammation.[15] It now seems that this occurs through stimulation of the vagus nerve, especially since a state of relaxed breathing occurs with both of them. In fact, anything that initiates what Harvard professor Herbert Benson calls the 'relaxation response', which includes meditation, yoga, prayer or *tai chi*, should activate the vagus nerve and thus slow the rate of ageing and offer us some protection from disease.

So, just as we are able to influence our heart rate through breathing and thinking, we can also influence the inflammatory response by the same process. It has even been suggested that the vagus nerve might be involved in some of the effects of acupuncture and prayer.[16]

Indeed, a 2002 study found that fever in rats produced by a bacterial endotoxin was significantly reduced by acupuncture and the elevated levels of interleukin-6 that accompanied the endotoxin exposure were quickly returned to normal.[17]

Another 2002 study found that attendance at religious services was associated with reduced levels of some pro-inflammatory cytokines in diabetic patients.[18] And a 2001 study of healthy people found that those who attended regular religious service had lower levels of pro-inflammatory cytokines and suggested that the services were protective against heart disease.[19] Most likely, the elevated, inspired or relaxed state experienced during the religious service stimulated the vagus nerve and thus reduced the cytokine levels.

There are also other natural ways in which you can stimulate the vagus nerve. Holding your breath for a few seconds does it, as does coughing. Even dipping your face in cold water has been shown to stimulate it. And if you feel like it, tensing your stomach muscles as if you were pushing for a bowel movement activates it!

★★★★★

So there is much more to compassion than sharing the feelings of another person and wishing them free of suffering. We unavoidably gain from it too. Compassion causes beneficial structural changes in the brain. It also impacts the immune system and stimulates the vagus nerve. This offers us a degree of protection from a number of medical conditions where body-wide inflammation is involved. So compassion helps us to live longer.

STORIES OF KINDNESS

Diffusing Anger

I was driving my car one day, heading towards the Forth Road Bridge, when I accidentally cut in front of another driver. He beeped his horn and hurled a number of expletives in my direction. He was really angry.

It was scary and upsetting, but I gradually composed myself. When I eventually reached the bridge I was surprised to see that the same driver was now behind me again, right behind me as I drove into the tollbooth. So I paid his toll charge for him.

About a half-mile further up the road, he drove alongside me. This time he had a large smile and greatly softened face and he mouthed the words, 'Thank you.' **Maureen**

A Share of Sales

In business, there is a severe lack of compassion. It's a dog-eat-dog world. There are decisions to be made based on financial outcomes and there's no room for heartfelt stuff. At least, that's what I thought until we hired a new recruit named Willie.

I was his boss. We were working in sales and both of us had to bring in a certain amount of revenue every month or we would be sacked. I was doing OK, but he was soon struggling. To be honest, he wasn't the best salesman in the world, but he was a diamond of a man – rough, but worth his weight in gold.

Two months went by and there was a board meeting to decide who was worth keeping. I was OK. Willie, on the other hand, was not. His sales figures were way down and according to company policy he should have been given the boot. But when *it came to the board meeting, he was kept on. His sales figures had magically grown overnight.*

How? Well, I had a soft spot for Willie and, out of compassion, I had transferred some of my own sales onto his figures. I knew that he had a family to support and I didn't want him to be out of a job. No one knew, not even Willie himself.

What this taught me was that there is always room for compassion in business – you just have to look for the opportunity. **Peter**

CHAPTER 4

HOW KINDNESS CHANGES THE BRAIN

'You cannot do a kindness too soon, for you never know how soon it will be too late.'
Ralph Waldo Emerson

Whether you're being kind or showing compassion, you are changing your brain. In fact, you are *always* changing your brain, whatever you are doing. This is one of the most exciting neuro-science discoveries of the twenty-first century.

For a start, the brain changes as we move our muscles. For instance, if I were to move my little finger back and forth for an hour or two and then take an MRI scan of the area of my brain connected to my little finger, it would have changed. The small area that was once governing my little finger would now be a larger area, like a small forest that had expanded.

The brain also changes as we think. As 'out there' as it may sound, if I were to just imagine moving my little finger back and forth for an hour or two, an MRI scan would also reveal that the forest had grown, and by just as much as when I actually moved my finger.

The changeability of the brain is known as *neuroplasticity* and it is the means whereby a compassion meditation increases the thickness of the prefrontal cortex.[1] How does it work? If we were to zoom in on the brain while we were moving our little finger, we would see brain cells linking with other brain cells and passing information along the connections between them. As we think the same thought over a period of time, we actually create more connections in the brain. And the creation of new connections occurs in the part of the brain that processes the kinds of thought we're thinking. For instance, thinking compassionate thoughts creates millions of new connections on the left side of the frontal cortex of the brain, which is just above the left eye.

Taking another example, moving your right arm creates new connections in a section of the brain known as the motor cortex. Imagining moving your right arm does the same thing. And, strange as it may seem, imagining moving your right arm over and over again actually makes the muscles stronger. Cellular changes in the right arm occur because of thoughts *about* the right arm.

So, every thought, regardless of what it is about, brings about chemical reactions in your brain and, when it is repeated often, structural changes too. You can be pretty certain that all your inspirations, motivations, loves, fears, hopes and dreams, and even your typical body language, are wired into your brain in the form of connections between cells. These connections become so extensive over time that they even wire into 3-D networks, or circuits, as they are often called.

Acts of kindness, then, find their way into the chemistry and structure of our brain. If kindness becomes a habit, we can significantly alter the wiring of our brain. In fact, as we will examine later, the brain is already wired for kindness. But we are always adding to and changing that wiring.

Throughout life, as we learn new things, grow, change our minds and even change our habits, new networks of new brain connections are laid down and old networks unravel. This neuroplasticity occurs right up until the very last seconds of our lives. One of the benefits of it is that it actually allows the brain to get over injury and disease, as healthy brain cells compensate for damaged ones by sprouting new connections to take over some of their communications or pass the information through the brain by a slightly different route.

To take a simple example, say a person wanted to learn a new skill like playing a musical instrument. The neural circuits involved in coordinating their finger movements and hearing the precise sounds made would initially be quite small and ill-defined. But after a few weeks of practice, more connections would have been laid down and the circuits would have become much more defined. Many, many millions of brand new connections between brain cells would have sprouted, like newly planted saplings growing into a thriving forest.

In one neuroplasticity study, conducted by scientists at the University of Regensburg in Germany, volunteers learned to juggle three balls over a three-month period. When MRI scans were taken of their brains, the area that processed visual movement had grown larger. Millions of new connections had sprouted, increasing the size of the circuits needed for coordinating the juggling movements.[2]

So, when you change yourself in any way, you change your brain. And if you bring more kindness into your life then you will bring about chemical and structural changes to your brain that will help to establish kindness circuits. You will wire your brain for more kindness.

What does this mean for us in daily life? It means that we can change our habits. We needn't be at the mercy of thoughts like 'That's just my personality' or 'It's in my genes so there's nothing I can do about it.' Negative habits can be replaced with positive ones, selfish ones with kind ones, suspicion with trust, hostility with empathy and complaints with gratitude.

And it's not just the brain that changes as we change our thoughts and behaviour. The body changes, too, at the cellular level.

NEUROPEPTIDES

The way it works is that chemicals known as neuropeptides are continually manufactured in an area of the brain known as the hypothalamus. From there, many flow into the pituitary gland and are released into the bloodstream in response to our thoughts and emotions.

As these 'molecules of emotion', as Candace Pert, one of the scientists who pioneered the study of the mind–body connection, calls them, circulate around the bloodstream, they carry information to different parts of the body. Many of them pass this information into cells by fitting into receptors on the surface of the cells. Think of a child's toy where different-shaped blocks have to be fitted into different-shaped holes. There's often a circle, a triangle, a square and a wavy shape. The neuropeptide is the block and the receptor is the hole that it fits into. The cell is the table or other object that the holes are on. In biological terms, when the block fits into the hole, i.e. when the neuropeptide fits into the receptor, information is passed to the cell.

Another way to think of it, less colourful but slightly more accurate, is to think of the neuropeptide as a space shuttle. For it to dock onto a space station, which would be the cell for this analogy, its docking port has to be the same shape as the docking port on the station. When it docks, an astronaut could walk into the space station and enter new information into its computers. In the same way, a neuropeptide fits into its receptor and passes information to the cell, entering new instructions into its 'computer', which, for this analogy, is the DNA. So some of the information activates or deactivates genes.

In this way, our thoughts, attitudes, beliefs and emotions impact us at the cellular and genetic level. It's happening constantly, throughout the brain and body. It's actually impossible to disentangle your mind from your body. The effects of your thinking and feeling, your loves and fears, your attitudes, behaviour and relationships are all felt at the genetic level.

That thoughts affect our genes is not as sensational a claim as you might think. It is a perfectly natural process that occurs 24 hours a day, 365 days a year in the brain and body. It's merely that few people realize it. This is, in fact, why protein or hormone levels in the body can rise and fall in response to a thought. When a signal in the form of a neuropeptide reaches a cell and sticks onto a receptor, information enters the cell and it might tell a gene to switch on. Thus, a hormone, protein or enzyme is formed and released from the cell. So, as our minds enter periods of, say, stress or calm, genes are switched on or off and the corresponding hormone or protein levels rise or fall in response.

To take a real example, stress, for instance, causes some genes to switch off (or turn down their activity) that are actually required to repair the body when it is damaged. In one study into wound-healing following an operation, over 170 genes were affected by stress and around 100 of these, some of which were supposed to make proteins to facilitate wound healing, were turned down. The wound, therefore, took over 40 per cent longer to heal.[3]

The other side of stress is calm. It is no surprise to learn, then, that meditation turns down genes that produce stress hormones. In 2008, scientists actually showed that the relaxation response, which is the body's physiological response to meditation, yoga, *tai chi* or any relaxing exercise that involves slow, regular breathing, impacted 1,561 genes after only eight weeks practice.[4]

Thoughts of kindness or compassion have their own neuropeptides too. One that is highly important is oxytocin, and we will look at it more closely in the next chapter.

STORIES OF KINDNESS

Strength by Sharing

Several years ago I was walking the Inca Trail in Peru as part of a group of 17 people. As we left the first morning to set off on a full day's walk to camp, our organizer told us to leave our rucksacks for the porters, as several had been hired to carry our stuff. Although there were 17 of us, there were only about a half-dozen porters.

A few miles into the walk I was stunned as these small men started to overtake us carrying three or four rucksacks each, all strapped together. I saw mine on one of their backs, along with two others and a large Calor gas cylinder. It was being carried by a small, thin man and his legs were shaking. I thought my rucksack was heavy enough on its own.

As we walked up through the mountain trail, which was often steep, I could see some of the porters were really struggling. I felt sad that they were having to do this and shared my feelings with one of my friends. We decided to help out by carrying our own rucksacks the next day.

The following day, after a few miles, our guide came alongside us. He was Peruvian. He wondered why we were carrying our own bags, so I explained that I couldn't bear to see these poor men carrying our bags all these miles up the mountain.

The guide then explained that if everyone followed my example, the company that hired the porters would start to hire fewer of them. For some of these men, he explained, this was the only work they could get. And even though it kept them away from their families for four or five days a week, it still meant they could provide for their wives and children. He assured me that I was doing them a favour by allowing them to carry my bags. So I handed in my rucksack the next morning along with everyone else.

But I still felt I wanted to help in some way. On that day, the third of the four-day trek, it was around 80 degrees and everyone was hot and stopping briefly every mile or so. It was also the hardest day of the trek, as we were making our way towards the highest point of Dead Woman's Pass at around 14,000 feet. Many of us were chewing coca leaves to combat altitude sickness.

The porters didn't have any water or coca leaves, so whenever one of them passed me or I passed one of them, I'd offer him some water and coca leaves. All of them gratefully accepted and I was warmed by the smiles of gratitude on their faces.

I soon realized that I definitely wouldn't have enough water for myself to make it all the way up, but I figured that the porters needed it more than me, with all that they were carrying.

Yet as we continued to walk and I continued to share my water and coca leaves, as well as the few chocolate bars and other snacks I was carrying, I felt strong. In fact, the more I gave away, the stronger I felt.

When we eventually reached the top, I felt fantastic, better than I had done in years. I felt exhilarated. I was definitely not tired, or thirsty or hungry, as many of my friends were.

Giving away what I thought I needed caused me not to need it at all. I gained all the strength I needed from sharing. It was a big lesson.

CHAPTER 5

OXYTOCIN IN THE BRAIN

'Remember there's no such thing as a small act of kindness. Every act creates a ripple with no logical end.'
Scott Adams

Oxytocin is a neuropeptide made up of nine amino acids. It is made in the brain in an area known as the hypothalamus and new studies show that it is also made in the heart. In the brain, it is delivered from the hypothalamus to the pituitary gland, where it is stored for release into the bloodstream. When released, it travels around the body and carries out different roles, serving as a hormone.

It is also made in the foetus and the placenta and one of its roles is to stimulate contractions in pregnant women. In fact, this is what it is best known for and it is used widely around the world to induce labour. Almost half of all women in the USA, for instance, are given a commercial form of oxytocin known as pitocin for this.

Oxytocin also causes the release of milk from the mammary gland in lactating women. Levels rise when mothers touch their newborn babies, or even look at them, and this stimulates milk flow. Some new mothers actually receive oxytocin to trigger the release of breast milk. Almost every mother in Israel receives oxytocin treatment after giving birth.

It is produced in copious quantities when we connect with others and when we're in love. It has even been affectionately called the 'love hormone'. Levels of oxytocin rise when we have sex, especially during orgasm. Even simple loving touch stimulates the release of a flood of oxytocin into the bloodstream. In fact, any sense of connection with another person, or an animal, produces oxytocin.

When you perform an act of kindness, especially where it involves face-to-face contact with the person involved, the momentary connection between you generates oxytocin in both you and them. In a sense, it could also be called a 'molecule of kindness'. And when you hug someone, oxytocin flows through both of you. Indeed, it has even been called the 'cuddle chemical'.

TO TRUST OR NOT TO TRUST

As well as being released into the bloodstream, oxytocin projects into the brain and moulds our behaviour. One of the simple consequences of this is that the more oxytocin in the brain, the more trusting we are. Our barriers go down. We become less shy and more confident, which helps us to make connections that we might not ordinarily make. One study even showed that people looked at other people's eyes in photographs for longer after they had been given a burst of oxytocin.[1]

Trust is a big issue in business. Standard economics tells us that we are inherently untrustworthy, selfish creatures and don't consider the feelings of others. The 'greed is good' philosophy is considered acceptable. Economics models base predictions on a 'self first' philosophy. But these models fail to describe the richness of human behaviour, the fact that, at times, we're more likely to be selfless, even at significant cost to ourselves, and we do care how others feel. Real interactions in daily life and in business often involve sharing and cooperation.

Oxytocin research is beginning to show us that we are indeed wired to show kindness, to commit selfless acts, to cooperate and share and trust. It's showing us that we have warm hearts and that our brains are wired for trust and generosity. Some of this research is coming from the growing field of neuroeconomics, which looks at what happens in the brain when we make economic decisions.

One way that trust is measured in economics research is by studying people playing what is known as the 'Trust Game'. In this game, one player, called the investor, has, say, £10 and has to decide whether to share it with the other player, called the trustee, who also has £10. The rules of the game are that whatever sum the investor shares is automatically tripled.

Let's say the investor shares the whole £10. It is immediately tripled and is now in the hands of the trustee. Now the trustee is faced with a decision. Do they keep the £30, plus their own £10, and go off with £40, leaving the investor with nothing – a selfish act? It's a win for them but not for the investor. Or do they repay the trust they've been shown by choosing to share some of the £30 with the investor? Maybe if they give £20 back then they can both walk away with £20.

Trusting turns out to be the most profitable solution for everyone in the long term. But from time to time it also leaves the investor open to the possibility of being betrayed. In the Trust Game, when we trust, we are relying on the good nature of the trustee.

Now, let's say the investor is betrayed. If they have to play further rounds of the game, chances are they will hedge their bets a little and be less generous in what they offer as an investment. This is indeed what economics games show.

But what if oxytocin, which increases trust, is flowing like a river in the investor's brain? Fascinating new research shows that if oxytocin is squirted up the nose of an investor before they play the first round of the Trust Game, even if they are betrayed they will still share the same amount as they did at the start.[2]

Altered brain activity was shown in a recent neuroeconomics study that examined the brain while participants played the Trust Game. In the study, conducted by scientists at the University of Zurich, 49 participants played the Trust Game 12 consecutive times. Some received a squirt of oxytocin before they started playing and the rest were given a squirt of placebo instead, which was a basic salt-water solution. Then, as the game was played, the scientists took MRI scans of the investors' brains while they made their decisions about how much to invest and whether to trust or not.

After the first six rounds, the investors were given feedback on their investments and were told that their trust had been betrayed several times (around 50 per cent of the time, in fact). This derailed the participants who had received placebos before they played the game. In the following six rounds, they invested much less. Their trust had been betrayed, so they were less trusting. But the participants who had received a squirt of oxytocin invested the same amount as they had done in the first rounds, even though they had been betrayed.

The fMRI scans showed that the key areas of the brain affected were the amygdala, an area that is associated with fear and anxiety, and the dorsal striatum, an area that guides future behaviour based on positive feedback. Participants who received oxytocin had much lower activity in the amygdala, equating to less fear of being betrayed again or less fear of the financial effects of betrayal. And they had much lower activity in the dorsal striatum, too, meaning that they didn't need to rely on positive results to make future decisions.

When oxytocin is flowing, knowing that we've just been betrayed doesn't change our trusting behaviour. Economic theory doesn't take this into account, however, and for this reason some of the economic models fail in evaluating the potentials of human behaviour. All we need is the right stimulation.

Few would argue, for example, with the fact that we tend to be more trusting, more caring and more generous when we're in love. This is a time when oxytocin is flowing through our brain and body. And we see the best in people, even those who have hurt us in the past. We are more forgiving and accepting. We trust people more. The fear of betrayal doesn't register with us in the same way. For us, the world is a beautiful place.

At the chemical level, the reason for this behaviour lies in how oxytocin impacts the brain. It fits into receptors in cells in the brain, and when it does, it can turn activity up or it can turn it down, just as a light bulb can be turned up or down. It can even stimulate the flow of other chemicals.

Most people assume that too much trust makes no economic sense, that we should play our cards close to our chest, but neuroeconomic and other studies are painting a very different picture and standard economic assumptions are now being overturned. It turns out that trusting others is the most profitable solution. Yes, sometimes we will be betrayed, but trusting is best for everyone in the end.

This can even be seen in national economies. Exciting research shows that they also fare better when citizens trust each other more. When polling for levels of trust across large populations by asking citizens, 'Would you say that most people can be trusted or would you say that you can't be too careful in dealing with people?' economists find that levels of trust in nations are strikingly related to their per capita output growth and the individual wealth of their citizens.

For example, research by Paul J. Zak, of Claremont Graduate University, and Stephen Knack, of the World Bank, showed that for every 15 per cent increase in trust, per capita output growth of the nation increased by 1 per cent for every year afterwards. In financial terms for individuals, that equated to a $430 per person increase in wealth.

It seems that trust does make excellent economic sense. In a paper called 'Building Trust: Public Policy, Interpersonal Trust, and Economic Development', written for a Supreme Court economic review in the USA, Zak and Knack went on to show that interpersonal trust was not only good for economic development, but that it was absolutely necessary.[3]

Trusting may mean that we get bitten from time to time, but we will usually win in the long term. The research by Zak and Knack showed that in nations where there were very low levels of trust, people could get caught in a poverty trap because with low trust came low investment. This led them into a downward economic spiral.

This is slightly concerning, because it seems that trust is decreasing in the world. In the UK, for instance, the level of trust was 56 per cent in 1959, but by 1998 it was down to 30 per cent. It's a similar picture in the USA. Trust fell from 56 per cent to 33 per cent over the same period.[4]

So we need to trust more, for the good of all. What's the best way to start? Although oxytocin generates trust, the solution isn't to spray everyone with it, even though some businessmen have been known to spray it in the boardroom to increase the likelihood of a sale! There are, however, many simple ways in which we can generate it. Giving someone a hug, for instance, increases oxytocin. Who would have believed that more hugs could be equated to the increased wealth of a nation?

What the world needs is for each of us to take the leap of faith required to reach out our hands in trust, even when we could be betrayed, and in forgiveness, in compassion and in kindness. Change starts in our own hearts and minds. And perhaps it starts with some simple acts of kindness.

Could we be kind and not be repaid, or trust and be betrayed? Of course! But that is always a risk in life. So should we always hedge our bets and play our cards close to our chest or should we put our faith blindly in people? Maybe we should meet ourselves somewhere in the middle. We should be intelligent and alert, but err on the side of kindness and trust if we want a win for ourselves, our countries and humanity.

SEEING PEOPLE DIFFERENTLY

Not only does oxytocin help us trust more but it is so good at reducing fear and anxiety, especially fear and anxiety about people and their behaviour, that it can help us change a negative opinion about someone, even turn an enemy into a friend. This is so important in life. Changing negative opinions about others starts us on the road to better-quality relationships, and these improve our health, as you will learn in a later chapter.

In a 27-person 2008 study conducted by scientists from University College London, the participants had to look at a number of faces while inside an MRI scanner. Some faces were preconditioned to produce fear in the participants. To create this fear, scientists gave the participants an electric shock when they looked at those faces. This produced activation in the amygdala, which we know is an area of the brain linked to fear and anxiety, and also the fusiform face area, which is related to recognizing facial identity. Together, these brain areas signal that a face equates to a threat of some kind.

After being shown the faces, the participants were taken out of the scanner and approximately half inhaled oxytocin spray and the other half a saltwater placebo. After 45 minutes, they all went back inside the MRI scanner and once again looked at the faces. Those in the placebo group reacted negatively to the faces that had had the shocks attached to them and gave them low likeability ratings. However, those who had received oxytocin had absolutely no adverse reaction to those faces and even rated them as likeable. Having turned down activity in the amygdala, oxytocin had deleted the negative reaction to the faces.

In the participants who had received the placebo, there was significant activation in the amygdala, indicating fear or an anxiety about the faces. However, in the oxytocin group there was no activation. Oxytocin had fit into oxytocin receptors in the amygdala and turned down its activity, producing a different feeling. In the placebo group, there was also significant activation in the fusiform face area, indicating a negative association with the faces. But this activation was again neutralized by oxytocin.[5]

This is what kindness can do. It can turn an enemy into a friend, at least in our own minds, which is where the change first needs to take place.

Other recent research has linked oxytocin to the recognition of faces, even when there's no threat involved. In a 2009 University of Zurich study published in the *Journal of Neuroscience*, 44 men were shown photographs of faces, landscapes and pictures. Before looking at the photos, 22 of them had inhaled a dose of oxytocin and the other 22 had inhaled a saltwater placebo.

The next day they were asked to look at more photographs. Some of these were new photographs, but some were ones they had seen the previous day. The men were asked to note if they had seen any of the photos before. Those who had received oxytocin were much better at remembering the faces they had seen the day before. As you would expect, there was no difference when they were viewing the landscapes or sculptures, because oxytocin relates to our connections with *people*.[6]

Since we generate oxytocin through our behaviour, this shows we can increase our ability to recognize people and even help ourselves get over negative opinions about others. And all we really need to do to start this all off is to be kind.

And have you noticed that when you feel good, when you're in love or you feel connected in some way, you find others more likeable and more attractive? Studies show that not only does oxytocin help us change negative feelings about people but it also causes us to find others more attractive.

In a study led by psychologist Angeliki Theodoridou, men and women received doses of oxytocin and then had to rate the attractiveness of a stranger. It was a double-blind placebo-controlled trial involving 96 men and women. Half received a dose of oxytocin and half got a placebo, which was a simple salt solution. Then they rated the attractiveness of 48 men and women. They also rated the trustworthiness of 30 men and women. Those who had had the oxytocin gave both men and women higher attractiveness ratings and also regarded them as more trustworthy than those who had received the placebo.[7]

Oxytocin even helps us read other people's emotions. A study at Rostock University in Germany involved 30 men who had to see how well they could read the emotions in the eyes of people in photographs. It reported that 20 of the men were much better at it after they received a dose of oxytocin.[8]

It has now been suggested that oxytocin could even help autistic people. Indeed, in a study led by Dr Eric Hollander of the Mount Sinai School of Medicine in New York involving autistic adults, it improved their recognition of emotions in a tone of voice. In the study, 15 adult autistic patients were given either oxytocin or placebo injections. Afterwards, those who had received oxytocin were much better at reading the emotions than the others. And the positive changes lasted for nearly two weeks.[9]

Scientists at the same university have now shown that oxytocin nasal sprays improve autistic patients' abilities to read and interpret facial expressions as well.[10]

So oxytocin helps us see others in a better light, remember them and even be better judges of their emotions. With it, we become more skilled at dealing with and interacting with people. And the key to generating it is to be kind.

YOU'LL WANT TO BE MORE GENEROUS

Although we produce oxytocin when we show kindness to others, it also makes us even more generous. It's a positive upward spiral.

A 2007 study carried out by scientists at the Center for Neuroeconomics Studies at Claremont Graduate University actually measured generosity. Participants played a game known as the 'Ultimatum Game'. In it, two participants were randomly paired to play together. One was assigned to the role of decision-maker 1 and the other decision-maker 2.

In a typical game, decision-maker 1 was given $10 in real money and had to decide whether to share some of it with the other decision-maker, just like in the Trust Game. But the key to this game was that decision-maker 2 didn't have to accept the sum, especially if they felt that it was too low. Prior to the game, they actually had to state the minimum amount they would accept, but decision-maker 1 wasn't told how much this was. But since an amount had been set, that meant that decision-maker 1 had to consider the feelings of decision-maker 2 when making an offer. When decision-maker 2 accepted the offer, they both walked away with their share. So if $3 was offered and was accepted, decision-maker 1 would have $7 and decision-maker 2 would have $3. But when the offer was rejected because it was too low, they both walked away with nothing.

Over several rounds, both players got a turn at being the first and second decision-makers. As they considered the feelings of the other person, the generosity of decision-maker 1 was reflected by how much they offered over the minimum acceptable amount.

In the games, 68 participants began by either inhaling a squirt of oxytocin (via a nasal inhaler) or a saltwater placebo. Starting with $10, the average decision-maker 1 offer in the oxytocin group was $4.86 and in the placebo group $4.03. The oxytocin group gave 21 per cent more.

The average minimum acceptable offer was approximately the same with oxytocin or the placebo: $2.97. While considering the feelings of decision-maker 2, those who received oxytocin therefore gave $1.89 more than the minimum acceptable offer ($4.86 minus $2.97), i.e. they were generous to the tune of $1.89. Those who received the placebo gave $1.06 more ($4.03 minus $2.97). Oxytocin made the decision-maker 1s 80 per cent more generous.[11]

In rounds of another game that the participants played, the 'Dictator Game', which was the same as the Ultimatum Game except that decision-maker 2 didn't get the choice whether to accept or reject an offer, oxytocin didn't make any difference to how much decision-maker 1 offered. This was because the first decision-maker didn't have to consider the other player.

When we have to consider another person's feelings, oxytocin ensures that we consider them highly. It makes us feel more connected with them, even more like them if we feel that they are low-power individuals.

$$\star\star\star\star\star$$

Overall, oxytocin can make us more trusting and more generous. It can enable us to feel closer to other people. It can help us see others in a better light and perhaps even turn enemies into friends. Thus, it can improve our mental and emotional health by impacting on the quality of our relationships and our interactions with each other.

These beneficial changes start in our own hearts. We ourselves need to step forward with acts of kindness. Then, as we connect with the people we help, oxytocin flows in our brain and enhances all of our other interactions and relationships.

There is so much that kindness can do for us. Few of us realize just how important it is. I like the way Henry James, the nineteenth-century American-British author, put it. He wrote: 'Three things in human life are important. The first is to be kind. The second is to be kind. The third is to be kind.'

And the benefits go far beyond improving our relationships with each other.

STORIES OF KINDNESS

The Best Policy

Recently I was in the Outlet Store at Tillicoultry. I picked up a small umbrella and a tablecloth, which I wanted to give as a present. I paid for the tablecloth but realized when I got home that I had not paid for the umbrella. I didn't want to trail back to the store, so I just posted off a cheque for the money, not expecting to hear any more about it.

Two weeks later I got a phone call from the store manager. He was completely astounded that I had sent a cheque, apologized for the lack of vigilance in the store, thanked me for my honesty and returned my cheque to me! Howzat! **Jo**

Roundabout Rage

There is a roundabout near where I live. It is always busy with traffic. A lot of the time people skip the queue in the lane that is my exit to go home and go to the front of the next lane, waiting to zoom off so they can squeeze into the exit lane before any cars from the correct lane. This used to so annoy me! 'Why can't they just wait like everybody else?!' I would yell. And every time that I was in the front of the queue and I suspected that this is what a car in the next lane was going to do, I would have my foot poised, ready to slam it down on the accelerator so that I would beat them to it and 'teach them a lesson'. 'Ha! That showed them!' I would proclaim, with my heart racing and my eyes popping out of my head.

However, one day, as I was sitting in the queue with two cars in front, there was a car in the next lane with the indicator on in the hope that someone would let it in. As the lights turned green, the two cars in front of me sped off, not letting the car in, and just as I was about to do the same, my foot eased off the accelerator. I realized that I didn't want to be stressed. I was calm and I wanted to stay that way. I didn't want my blood pressure to be raised and my anger levels to peak. So I gestured to the driver to say that it was OK, and he went in front. And I felt good! Much better than feeling as though my temples were going to pop from exasperation.

The guy then flashed his hazard lights as a thank-you. This made me feel even more brilliant! Since then I have let everyone go in front of me at that roundabout. It's no big deal in the grand scheme of things and I feel a zillion times better. **Elisa**

CHAPTER 6

WAYS TO PRODUCE OXYTOCIN

'Kindness in words creates confidence. Kindness in thinking creates profundity. Kindness is giving creates love.'
Lao-Tse

Oxytocin is called the 'love hormone' because it is produced when we're in love. It is also called the 'cuddle chemical' because it is produced when we hug. Any way, in fact, in which we feel a sense of connection with a person, a pet or even a spiritual deity produces oxytocin. It is produced when we have sex and during orgasm. It is even stimulated when we touch or stroke each other. Kindness and compassion also produce it, especially when they involve connecting with another person. So does socializing.

This chapter contains a rundown of some of these ways in which we can produce oxytocin, together with the science that proved it, and includes some unexpected ways too.

HOW TO INCREASE OXYTOCIN

1) GET INSPIRED

We produce oxytocin when we're inspired. In a recent study, using the fact that oxytocin stimulates lactation, psychologist Jonathon Haidt had 42 lactating women watch either an inspiring clip from *The Oprah Winfrey Show* or a comedy routine from *Seinfeld*. Around half of the women who watched *Oprah* leaked milk onto pads or fed their babies, but none of the women watching *Seinfeld* leaked milk. Only 15 per cent of the *Seinfeld* watchers fed their babies.

The scientists concluded that it was the sense of elevation from watching the *Oprah* clip, which was about a teacher saving a gang member from a life of violence, that produced oxytocin, and this led to the production of milk.[1]

2) EXPRESS EMOTIONS

A 2007 study led by scientists at the University of Groningen in the Netherlands showed that differences in how people expressed emotions were linked with oxytocin levels. It had previously been shown, and was quite well known, that reduced emotional expression was related to the susceptibility or rate of progression of breast cancer. Women who suppress emotion, especially negative emotion, are more at risk of developing breast cancer than those who easily express emotion, and for women who have breast cancer, the disease progresses fastest in those who suppress negative emotion. The scientists predicted that oxytocin would be involved in the process. Studies had shown that reduced expression of emotion could be related to rejection or separation, and recent research had shown that oxytocin was low in response to rejection or separation. Putting two and two together, the scientists thought that oxytocin might be low in those who didn't express emotion so well, and thus in women who did, it might actually protect them against the development of breast cancer, or at the very least slow its rate of progression.

In the study, healthy women were given either a placebo or cortisol and then blood was taken 70 minutes later. The cortisol was given to simulate the physiological experience of separation or rejection, which is known to increase cortisol.

To determine emotional expression, the scientists used a well-known emotional expression questionnaire containing statements like 'When I feel unhappy or miserable, I say what I feel', where agreement is considered an expression of emotions, and 'When I feel unhappy or miserable, I hide my unhappiness', which is considered holding feelings in.

When the blood was analysed, it was found that oxytocin levels were in proportion to the amount the women expressed themselves. Those who expressed themselves most had the highest oxytocin. It was suggested that oxytocin might also serve as a protection in some women from breast cancer.[2]

3) GET A MASSAGE

A 2008 UCLA study found that having a massage stimulated the release of oxytocin. Volunteers in the study either received a massage or had to wait in a room. Afterwards, they had to play an economics game that involved giving money to another player. The group of participants that had been massaged gave 243 per cent more money than the group who had waited. When the scientists analysed the blood of all the participants for oxytocin, it turned out that levels were elevated in those who had received the massage. It was concluded that the massage had produced the oxytocin.[3]

4) SUPPORT A LOVED ONE

Research by scientists from the University of North Carolina at Chapel Hill has shown that greater support from a partner is associated with higher blood oxytocin levels. The study involved 38 couples who were living together. They reported on how much they supported each other, which was considered an indicator of the closeness of their bond. It was found that those who had the greatest amounts of oxytocin in their blood were the ones who had reported the most warm contact.

Greater support was also associated with reduced blood pressure in the 10 minutes after warm contact and with lower levels of the stress hormone norepinephrine.

The scientists also pointed out that frequent positive partner interactions had cumulative long-term effects leading to consistently higher oxytocin levels and sustained lower blood pressure.[4]

Other research has indicated that even the anticipation of warm contact (a thought) might increase oxytocin levels.[5]

In a study published in 2008, warm touch itself was certainly found to increase oxytocin levels. Scientists from the Department of Psychology at Brigham Young University in Provo, Utah, conducted a four-week experiment involving 34 healthy married couples and measured oxytocin levels, blood pressure and stress hormone levels. Those who experienced the most warm touch had the highest levels of oxytocin.[6]

Warm touch can signal compassion – a compassionate hand on the arm or shoulder says, 'I am with you and I care.' It can also signal gratitude – a tiny shake of the hand as it embraces an arm or hand. And it can signal love – a squeeze that says, 'I love you and want to be close to you.' It can also signal kindness when we know another just needs support.

5) GIVE HUGS

In other University of North Carolina at Chapel Hill research, 59 married or partnered women were asked to keep a diary of the number of hugs they received over a set period of time. The scientists then took blood samples from each of the women and analysed them for oxytocin levels. It was shown that those who received the most hugs had the greatest baseline levels of oxytocin. They also had the lowest blood pressure and heart rates.[7]

You could say, 'A hug a day keeps the cardiologist away!'

6) STROKE A PET

When we can't be with another person, a pet is a great substitute. For many, in fact, it is much better. A loving pet is sometimes the only source of love in a person's life, and it can even save that life.

A large study examined the long-term survival of patients who had spent time in a cardiac unit. It found that what most determined survival was, of course, the extent of damage to the heart. But number 2 was having a pet. Four times fewer patients with a pet died within a year of being released from the cardiac unit than those without a pet.[8]

Stroking a dog or cat actually reduces our blood pressure, reduces stress and even wards off depression. It even reduces the blood pressure of our pets. They love to be loved, too, and they thrive on it. Stroking a pet also elevates our oxytocin levels. In fact, they almost double when we stroke our pets.

Playing with dogs also increases oxytocin. In one study, conducted by scientists at Azuba University in Japan, 55 dog owners played with their dogs for half an hour. Urine samples were taken at the start and again at the end to measure oxytocin levels.

The scientists also videotaped the play sessions to examine how much time the dogs spent gazing at their owners, splitting them into two groups: 'long gazers', who made eye contact for an average of 2.5 minutes during the half-hour, and 'short gazers', who only made eye contact for roughly 45 seconds. In this way, they were measuring the quality of relationship between dog and owner. The people who received longer gazes from their dogs were said to enjoy a better quality of relationship with them.

The study found that oxytocin levels went up by 20 per cent in the long gazers compared with a control group of dog owners who didn't play, whose oxytocin levels actually dropped a little.[9]

This rush of oxytocin is probably why playing with our pets can make us feel good, lifting our mood and even impacting depression and anxiety.

And it needn't just be pets. In a 1976 Harvard study, some nursing-home residents were given the responsibility of choosing a plant and caring for it. Other residents, in a control group, were told that tending plants was the nurses' responsibility. The study found that the enhanced responsibility of the residents (who usually had no responsibilities at all) was beneficial to them. The death rate of those who chose and cared for plants was around half the death rate of those who didn't.[10]

*****

So we produce oxytocin when we're in love, when we're hugging and when we have sex. A warm touch signalling compassion, gratitude or support also produces it. Massage generates it too.

It's produced when we're inspired, which might be when we're watching a movie, listening to music or appreciating art. It even flows when a person's behaviour inspires us.

When you're there for a friend or a friend is there for you, there is a flow of oxytocin. We also increase our levels of it if we express emotion regularly instead of holding it inside.

You can even stroke or play with a pet to produce oxytocin, and it will be flowing through the veins of your pet too.

Any way in which you connect with another being, any sense of connection whatsoever, produces oxytocin. Prayer produces oxytocin. Kindness, compassion and gratitude also produce it, especially when they are vehicles for us to bond with another person.

In the next chapter you will learn some of the healthy ways in which oxytocin impacts the body.

STORIES OF KINDNESS

Getting Home

When I was 17 and walking from the bus stop towards my home one day, I passed an old lady lying face down in a flowerbed. At first I didn't know what to do. Was she sleeping? Or drunk? Or was she hurt? I felt a wee bit of panic rise in my stomach, but I took a deep breath and approached her. As I knelt beside her, I could smell it – the air was thick with alcohol.

I asked if she was OK. She stirred and mumbled something I didn't understand. I gradually got her to sit up and asked her where she lived. It was a town a few miles away on the bus route that went along the very road we were on. The bus stop was on the other side of the road about 100 yards away, so I helped her to her feet, put my arm around her and helped her to walk in the direction of the bus stop.

When we were almost there, a police car drew alongside us. One of the policemen made a friendly comment to the woman. They knew her. Apparently this was quite common for her. They thanked me for helping her and took her inside the car. They were going to drive her home.

I thought that was really nice of them.

CHAPTER 7

OXYTOCIN, DIGESTION AND INFLAMMATION

'The value of a man resides in what he gives and not in what he is capable of receiving.'
Albert Einstein

Oxytocin receptors are now being found all over the body. It seems the more scientists look for them, the more they find them. A picture is emerging of oxytocin as a key component in a number of bodily systems, linking the mind and body in a way never before understood. This link goes some way to explaining why love and kindness and compassion are so good for our physical health. It seems that the entire body is healthier and works better when the love hormone flows.

GUT REACTIONS

On a very basic level, oxytocin helps us digest our meals. It plays a really important role in food digestion. In 2004, biopsies of human GI tracts (the system that takes in food, digests it, extracts the necessary nutrients and expels the waste matter, otherwise known as the gut) were taken at the Department of Surgery of Malmö University Hospital in Lund, Sweden, and analysed for the presence of oxytocin and oxytocin receptors. In nearly all biopsy segments, both oxytocin and oxytocin receptors were discovered.[1]

And they weren't there for no reason. First, it's been found that oxytocin promotes what is known as 'gastric motility', the contractions of the smooth muscles in the stomach that help digestion by moving food through the stomach and down into the intestines.[2] Through these muscle movements, the food is mixed, mashed and ground, becoming liquefied into a substance called chyme. The contractions then force the chyme down into the small intestine in 'gastric emptying'.

When we eat something, oxytocin is released into the bloodstream and helps in this process of mixing and grinding by stimulating the highly coordinated muscle contractions required.[3] When there is insufficient oxytocin, the muscle contractions become slow and uncoordinated and there is insufficient mixing and grinding and thus digestion slows down.

Next, oxytocin has been shown to stimulate gastric emptying.[4] To prove this, scientists gave ten healthy volunteers (five men and five women) a meal of rice pudding. Some also received a chemical called atosiban, which would stop oxytocin working, while others received a placebo. In the group that received the atosiban, the rate of gastric emptying was reduced by 37 per cent compared with some of the volunteers who had received the placebo. Blocking oxytocin meant that the rate of gastric emptying was significantly reduced, confirming the crucial role that oxytocin plays in the system.[5]

In the absence of adequate quantities of oxytocin, the entire digestive process slows down and can become problematic, a condition known as gastric *dys*motility. This can cause pain and discomfort. Children who suffer from recurring pain in the stomach have been found to have low levels of oxytocin in their bloodstream.[6]

A low level of oxytocin is sometimes even a complication of diabetes. In a 2009 study, scientists from the Department of Clinical Sciences at Malmö University Hospital, found that diabetic patients who had normal gastric motility had different concentrations of oxytocin in the GI tract from patients with dysmotility. The study involved 19 diabetic patients and found that those with normal gut functioning had a normal increase in oxytocin after eating a meal but those with slower gastric emptying had no increase. It was concluded that the oxytocin deficiency was responsible for the gastric dysmotility in the patients.[7]

The research also suggested that these digestive problems most likely had a hand in autonomic neuropathy, which also plagues some diabetic patients. Treating diabetic patients with concentrated doses of oxytocin is now being considered.

As a more long-term solution, some might find that just altering their way of relating to others might raise oxytocin levels naturally. For some it might mean working on the quality of their relationships, developing closer and more intimate bonds, or even just giving and receiving more hugs.

Oxytocin is also highly important in the colon. It helps the movement of matter though the colon by stimulating contractions, known as colonic peristalsis. In a 2004 study, 14 healthy female volunteers were given an infusion of lipid direct into their duodenum for 90 minutes. In addition, some of the women either received oxytocin in the infusion or a saline solution. During this time, the colonic motility was measured. In the women who received the oxytocin, there were almost six times more colon contractions per hour compared with those who received the saline (3.9 in the oxytocin group versus 0.7 in the saline group), demonstrating that oxytocin is crucial for the colonic elimination process.[8]

So it seems that the whole food-processing system needs oxytocin. And so our relationships with each other, which maintain oxytocin levels in the brain and body, actually play a role in how the body processes food. A kind attitude and healthy relationships equate to a healthy gut.

BE KIND TO YOUR BOWEL

IBS (irritable bowel syndrome) is a mild form of dysmotility. It is characterized by abdominal pain and discomfort associated with bowel habits. Most IBS patients have more sensitive intestines than healthy people and so become acutely aware of each contraction, which can be extremely painful. It is known as visceral sensitivity.

Oxytocin levels have been found to be lower in people suffering from IBS and it has been suggested that the low levels of oxytocin play a key role in these conditions.[9] Although this area hasn't been much studied, it might be that making more oxytocin is all that's needed.

It's funny, but in one of my previous books I suggested that a treatment for the symptoms of IBS could be to talk kindly to the bowel a few times a day. As silly as this might sound (you might want to be alone when you do it), this was born out of discussions with a few women who did just that and found that their symptoms all but disappeared fairly quickly. It seems that if we do speak kindly to the bowel, we might actually be raising oxytocin levels in the gut, which would, indeed, probably reduce the symptoms of IBS.

There's also a connection in some people between fibromyalgia, depression and IBS. In all of these conditions, patients have been found to have low levels of oxytocin in their bloodstream.[10]

When IBS patients are given oxytocin it does alleviate fibromyalgia pain and depression, as well as reduce visceral sensitivity. In a 1996 study, 26 IBS patients had a small flaccid bag placed in their descending colon along with a pressure sensor that measured the pressure in the colon as the bag was forced along it by colonic contractions. As the bag travelled along the colon, pain levels were recorded. Some patients also received oxytocin and some received a placebo. As expected, when pressure was high, pain was greatest. However, the pain threshold was greater for the patients who received oxytocin. The oxytocin had significantly reduced visceral sensitivity and thus pain.[11]

Similarly, for some people suffering from fibromyalgia or depression, independent of IBS, oxytocin might be the key to relieving their symptoms.

Research is now clearly showing that oxytocin is a bit of a dark horse, so to speak. It plays quite a number of important roles in the body that we never knew about until quite recently.

One of these is in reducing inflammation. Just as the vagus nerve plays a crucial role in the control of inflammation in the body, so it seems that oxytocin can too.

OXYTOCIN REDUCES INFLAMMATION

A few years ago, some scientists noticed that when women were lactating, i.e. when levels of oxytocin were very high, levels of some pro-inflammatory cytokines were lower than normal. A reasonable conclusion was that oxytocin had something to do with the reduction. A great deal of recent research has found this to be true.

As we learned earlier, inflammation is a necessary part of the healing process. But too much inflammation, which can accompany bacterial infections or chronic levels of stress, is damaging to the body. Research now shows that oxytocin reduces the inflammation caused by bacterial infections in humans.

This was reported in a groundbreaking 2008 paper published by scientists at the Medical University of Vienna in the *American Journal of Physiology, Endocrinology and Metabolism*. It was a placebo-controlled study involving ten healthy men. They were all injected with oxytocin and an endotoxin, which is the disease-causing part of a bacterium. Typically, if we are injected with a small amount of endotoxin, we develop fever and inflammation. Indeed, in an early part of the experiment there was a fast increase in the levels of several pro-inflammatory cytokines (including interleukin-6 and TNF-α) when the bacterial endotoxin was injected on its own. However, when oxytocin was injected at the same time as the endotoxin, the levels of pro-inflammatory cytokines were much lower.[12]

Interestingly, when part of the experiment was repeated in test tubes instead of the human body, the oxytocin didn't have the same effects. The scientists suggested that this was because it was also acting on the brain and might be stimulating the vagus nerve, tickling it, so to speak. Indeed, research back in late 1980s and early 1990s showed that oxytocin does actually increase activation of the vagus nerve.[13]

Oxytocin might thus even be used as a treatment for severe infections, as the authors of the study pointed out. The levels they used in their experiments were much higher than normal physiological levels. Just like stimulating the vagus nerve, injections of high doses of oxytocin could be used to control severe infections like sepsis and protect against damage to the entire body. Indeed, several studies have now shown that oxytocin protects against multiple organ damage due to severe infections.

Also, just as compassion or natural stimulation of the vagus nerve through, say, meditation could stop the dripping tap of pro-inflammatory cytokines, so oxytocin could do the same thing. So we can add love, making love, kindness, hugs, warm touch, gratitude, inspiration and connection with other people to our toolkit for reducing inflammation in the body and thus keeping ourselves healthier and even helping ourselves to live longer.

It is likely that when we have sufficient levels of oxytocin in our bloodstream, inflammation is kept to a minimum and the likelihood of inflammation-linked disease is kept low. This would mean that good-quality relationships are good for our health because they maintain good levels of oxytocin. And, as you will learn later on, this is exactly what research has discovered.

Similarly, our other natural methods of producing oxytocin, like being kind to each other, would serve as an overall daily tonic in protecting us from many diseases that spawn from inflammation, by nipping them in the bud before they can develop into anything problematic. It is amazing what kindness can do for you!

OXYTOCIN AND CANCER

It is well known that inflammation plays a role in many types of cancer. Recent research, for instance, has identified a strong link between inflammation and colon cancer. As oxytocin reduces inflammation, it might also offer some protection against colon cancer and other cancers that have an inflammation link.

The role of oxytocin in cancer, however, is not yet fully understood. Many studies show that it reduces the growth rate of tumours. For instance, in lab trials it has been shown to suppress the growth of non-small cell lung tumours[14] and in other studies it has reduced the growth rate of a variety of cancers such as ovarian, endometrial, bone, astrocytoma (which is a type of brain tumour) and neuroblastoma (which is the most common type in children, where it most frequently forms in the adrenal glands).[15] It is possible that in these cases it is working by reducing inflammation, although other mechanisms have been proposed too.

Similarly, in breast cancer, as we learned in the last chapter, some scientists have linked emotional expression with the development of the cancer and its rate of progression, and oxytocin might offer some protection against it.[16]

There are, however, a few other studies that have witnessed an increase in the growth rate of tumours in the presence of oxytocin. Yet it seems that these involve cancers where hormones play a large role and can be out of balance. One study, for instance, found that in the presence of normal hormone levels, oxytocin suppressed tumour growth in the prostate. But when the hormones were out of balance, oxytocin could increase tumour growth.[17]

The research that discovered this was led by scientists in the Department of Clinical Science at the University of Bristol and published in 2007. The scientists found that oxytocin had no effect on the growth rate of malignant cells when they were grown in the lab alone. But when the cells were grown together with cells of connective tissue (stromal cells) and gonadal steroids, which is an environment more like real conditions in the prostate, oxytocin actually reduced the growth rate of the malignant cells at normal physiological concentrations. Under normal conditions, then, oxytocin seemed to reduce tumour growth.

However, in another part of the experiment, it stimulated the growth of metastatic cancer cells (PC3 cells) when in the presence of testosterone.

Scientists have suggested that in prostate growth and prostate cancer it is the imbalance in the regulation of oxytocin by male steroid hormones (androgens) that is responsible for the growth.

Overall, in healthy people, when hormones are in balance, oxytocin may be constantly working to keep cancer at bay and to reduce any cancer that has a link with inflammation, which includes abdominal, liver, colorectal, ovarian and pancreatic cancer, along with some lymphomas and many others.

However, perhaps the most powerful health-giving effects of oxytocin are reserved for the heart. The next chapter will explore its many roles in keeping our hearts beating for longer.

STORIES OF KINDNESS

An Unexpected Gift

Back in 1981, when my sister was terribly ill, in fact dying, and my elderly parents were fretting about her, a stranger turned up at the door and thrust an envelope at us containing £200. The only message was: 'I expect your phone bills are high at the moment.' (My sister was in Canada and my parents were in Scotland.)

My father was moved to tears. **Jo**

A Kind Translator

My husband and I were in Nice after a night out and were waiting to get the last train to a town about ten miles away that we were staying in. We were on the platform when an announcement was made that we assumed meant that the platform was being changed, though we didn't totally understand it. We really should have learned to speak French a little better!

We thought we'd follow everyone else, but some people moved to one platform and some to a different one altogether. Some even stayed where they were. We were panicky because the train was due any minute.

Then a young Englishman who could see our distress explained what was happening and told us to follow him to the correct platform. As luck would have it, he was staying in the same town as we were.

We chatted with him all the way to the town, then he got off with us and went out of his way to ensure that we got safely to our hotel.

I love it when kindness comes at the most unexpected times. I almost felt that someone was watching over us that night. **Leigh**

CHAPTER 8

OXYTOCIN AND THE HEART

'You give but little when you give of
your possessions. It is when you give of
yourself that you truly give.'

Kahlil Gibran

We know that oxytocin makes us more generous and more trusting, behaviour that we might usually associate with the heart. This behaviour actually comes about from the effects of oxytocin in the brain, but a number of recent stories show that it does also affect the heart.

Evidence gathered in the 1990s began to point towards a role in the heart with the discovery, by scientists at the Institute of Drug Discovery and Research in the Yamanouchi Pharmaceutical Company, that oxytocin bound to receptors in the human aorta, the largest blood vessel in the body.[1]

And in 1999, scientists from the IWK Grace Health Center in Halifax, Canada, found that oxytocin also bound to receptors in the right atrium of the heart.[2]

In the same year, scientists at the Case Western Reserve University School of Medicine, in Cleveland, found that oxytocin bound to receptors in the aorta and pulmonary artery and to cells from the umbilical vein.[3]

More recent research has now discovered the multiple effects that oxytocin has when it binds to receptors in the heart and throughout the cardiovascular system. As we will see, research now clearly shows that it is cardioprotective – that is, it protects the heart from damage.

OXYTOCIN REDUCES BLOOD PRESSURE

Oxytocin interacts with cells along the walls of blood vessels and causes those cells to relax. When this happens, the blood vessels (arteries, veins, capillaries) widen, or dilate, in what is known as vasodilation. The outcome of this is that blood pressure comes down because there is less resistance from the walls of the vessels as blood flows through them.

Think of it like water flowing through a narrow hose. The water tap is set on high to force the water through the hose. Then imagine that the hose widens. It is now much easier for the water to get through, so there's less pressure in the hose. In the same way, oxytocin widens the 'hose' of our arteries, veins and capillaries, relaxing them and reducing our blood pressure.

So, when oxytocin is flowing, the entire cardiovascular system is relaxing. This is why, when you feel love, it's good for your heart and is perhaps why kindness and compassion give us a warm feeling in the chest.

On a chemical level, when oxytocin binds to receptors on the walls of the blood vessels, it causes them to make nitric oxide, and that is responsible for vasodilation. As we learned in Chapter 3, nitric oxide is one of the major factors in ageing, or at least not having enough of it is. As we age, levels tend to drop and this also impacts vascular tone, which refers to the capacity of our blood vessels to dilate. But since oxytocin stimulates the production of nitric oxide, it may even be helping us to live longer by keeping the cardiovascular system healthy and toned.[4]

Oxytocin also binds to receptors on heart-muscle cells and causes them to release a peptide called atrial natriuretic peptide (ANP), which is also a vasodilator and sometimes acts to slow the heart. Therefore oxytocin reduces blood pressure in two ways, both through dilating the blood vessels.[5]

OXYTOCIN SOFTENS OUR ARTERIES

A groundbreaking 2008 study showed that oxytocin also protects us against hardening of our arteries, a condition known as atherosclerosis.[6]

The scientists were studying the effects of oxidative stress on the cardiovascular system and the immune system, and the subsequent development of atherosclerosis. Oxidative stress is the name for excess free radicals that go on to damage the body. Free radicals, otherwise known as reactive oxygen species, are oxygen atoms missing a partner. Therefore they will covet their neighbour's wife, so to speak, by stealing a partner (atom) from anywhere in the body, including cells and DNA, which damages the cells and DNA. They are known to age the body and they accelerate the progress of many diseases, including cardiovascular disease and cancer. This is why antioxidants are so important. Part of what an antioxidant does is supply a partner to the free radical so that it relaxes and no longer steals one from cells or DNA.

In the study, performed at the Behavioural Medicine Research Center and Department of Psychology at the University of Miami, human vascular cells were incubated either in the presence of oxytocin or in the absence of it, for comparison purposes. In the cell cultures containing oxytocin, levels of oxidative stress were reduced by 24–48 per cent.

In another part of the experiment, the scientists discovered oxytocin receptors on cells of the immune system known as monocytes and macrophages, so they examined the effects of oxytocin on oxidative stress in these cells too. They found that it reduced oxidative stress in the immune cells by approximately the same amount as it did in the vascular cells. Thus, the study showed that oxytocin protects us against atherosclerosis by keeping oxidative stress out of the equation.

In a sense, as love and kindness makes our spiritual hearts go soft, the oxytocin that then flows through our arteries keeps them soft too. When we harden ourselves to others and the world, and reduce the flow of oxytocin to a drip, so we harden on the inside too.

The fact that oxytocin seems to reduce oxidative stress even suggests that it plays a role in keeping us young, as oxidative stress is known to accelerate the ageing process. It is also known to be involved in heart failure, myocardial infarction, Alzheimer's disease, chronic fatigue and Parkinson's disease. So love, kindness and connection with others offer a degree of protection against all of these conditions.

Inflammation also contributes to atherosclerosis. In another part of the study, the scientists introduced the vascular cells and immune cells to a bacterial endotoxin, which is known to increase levels of interleukin-6. In cell cultures containing no oxytocin, interleukin-6 levels were high, but in the cultures containing oxytocin, the levels were reduced by 56 per cent in the immune cells and 26 per cent in the vascular cells.

We learned earlier that oxytocin stimulates, or tickles, the vagus nerve to reduce levels of pro-inflammatory cytokines, but these experiments were done in cell cultures with no vagus nerve. So oxytocin can not only work with the vagus nerve but can also reduce inflammation by acting on vascular cells and immune cells directly.

The scientists concluded that oxytocin played a much larger role in keeping us healthy than ever previously imagined because it not only kept the heart and vascular system healthy but also impacted the immune system. Love and kindness, then, in producing oxytocin, have a much greater influence on our health than we ever thought. When they are not present, and oxytocin levels are therefore lowered, we become more susceptible to diseases of the heart and immune system.

Several studies have indeed previously linked hostile behaviour, which would ensure low levels of oxytocin, with atherosclerosis and other cardiovascular diseases.

One such study was performed by scientists at the University of Utah and published in 2006.[7] It involved 150 married couples, who were asked to discuss a topic from their marriage while being videotaped. When they watched the videotapes, the scientists categorized the couples according to how they behaved towards one another. At one end of the extreme were those couples who were most hostile towards each other and at the other end were those who were most loving and kind.

Those who were most hostile were found to have greater levels of atherosclerosis. Through their own behaviour, they had turned their oxytocin tap down, thus making themselves more susceptible to atherosclerosis by allowing oxidative stress and inflammation to act on their blood vessels.

The couples who were the most loving and kind towards each other had the lowest levels of atherosclerosis. Their loving behaviour would have produced oxytocin and this would have protected them by keeping oxidative stress and inflammation low.

In another study, scientists at Ohio State University were examining the effects of a high-fat and cholesterol diet on the development of atherosclerosis in rabbits.[8] As expected, the fatty diet caused atherosclerosis. However, one group of rabbits had 60 per cent less atherosclerosis than all the rest. This was confusing at first and the scientists checked out every possible cause for their better health. It was only when a new technician admitted that she had taken these rabbits out of their cages at night and lovingly stroked them that things became clearer. It was the stroking of the rabbits that was reducing their atherosclerosis levels.

The scientists repeated the study, but this time they made the stroking of some rabbits an actual part of it. And just as before, the rabbits that were stroked had 60 per cent less atherosclerosis than all the rest.

Studies in humans show that hugs produce oxytocin, and all vertebrates produce oxytocin or something very similar. So it is likely that lovingly stroking the rabbits produced oxytocin in their bodies and this was reducing the oxidative stress and inflammation caused by the high-fat and cholesterol diet.

So oxytocin is actually protective against this form of cardiovascular disease. Giving someone a hug, then, not only protects your heart but theirs too. What a gift!

LOVE CREATES NEW BLOOD VESSELS

Angiogenesis is the name for the growth of new blood vessels. It is a vital process that is crucial in wound repair, growth and the development of the human body. Studies have now shown that when new blood vessels are forming, thin layers of cells lining the entire vascular system are stimulated. These cells, known as endothelial cells, contain copious quantities of oxytocin receptors and thus respond to the presence of oxytocin.

In research published in 2009, scientists from the Università degli Studi di Milano in Milan, Italy, studied the effect of oxytocin on a special type of endothelial cell known as a human umbilical vein endothelial cell (HUVEC). HUVECs are used widely in biology as a standard for studying endothelial cells. By studying how oxytocin affected them, the scientists could get a fairly accurate picture of how cells throughout the entire vascular system would respond to it. In the study, when the HUVECs were immersed in oxytocin, it bound to receptors on the HUVECs and then capillary-like structures grew out from the HUVECs. Oxytocin had promoted angiogenesis.[9]

Since angiogenesis is an important part of wound healing, it is easy to see the importance of oxytocin in healing and therefore how our relationships with each other must affect the way our wounds heal. We know that stress and emotional conflict prolong the healing of emotional wounds, but it seems that they prolong the healing of physical wounds too.

Indeed, several studies have shown that wounds take longer to heal when people are under stress or amid an emotional conflict – times when oxytocin levels are low. In a 2005 study, for instance, scientists from Ohio State University found that in a sample of 42 couples, those who showed the most conflict behaviour healed at only 60 per cent of the rate of everyone else.[10]

In a 2004 study at the same university, social interaction, which produces oxytocin, was shown to speed up the healing of skin wounds. In the same study, administering oxytocin to socially isolated hamsters also speeded up wound healing.[11]

And in a 2009 study conducted by scientists at Harvard University and Massachusetts General Hospital, administering oxytocin to rats speeded up the healing of burn wounds. Rearing the rats in a social group, which also produces oxytocin, had the same effect.[12]

One of the key growth factors in angiogenesis is known as vascular endothelial growth factor (VEGF). It promotes capillary growth. One of the key findings in the angiogenesis study was that oxytocin promoted angiogenesis almost to the same extent as VEGF.

It seems that both oxytocin and VEGF contribute to angiogenesis when wounds are healing. But oxytocin, in responding to our emotions and behaviour, explains why wound healing is influenced by our emotions and behaviour.

Our thoughts, feelings, actions, behaviour and relationships, then, all impact how we heal. No longer can we disconnect ourselves from our physical healing. We must acknowledge that we always play a role. The way we are feeling might just be the deciding factor in our recovery. And kindness makes us heal faster.

REPAIRING A BROKEN HEART

There's been a lot of excitement in cardiology recently with the discovery that heart-muscle cells can replace themselves, something that was previously thought to be impossible. It is well known that heart-attack patients who make significant dietary and other lifestyle changes often enjoy healthy lives. But evidence now suggests that in such cases some of the heart-muscle and vascular damage might actually have been repaired.

Some of this evidence comes from studying the effects of exercise on heart-attack patients. A 2004 study, for instance, found that almost 90 per cent of heart patients who regularly cycled were free of heart problems within one year after they started exercising, compared with only 70 per cent who had received a stent.[13]

A 2007 study by scientists at Leipzig University in Germany found that people who had serious heart failure but rode a bike for up to 30 minutes a day for four months produced new stem cells in their bone marrow. In addition, they also had more small blood vessels in their muscles compared with those who didn't exercise, who had no change in their blood vessels or muscles.[14]

The scientists suggested that endothelial progenitor cells, which are a type of stem cell that is believed to travel out of the bone marrow in response to ischaemia (damage to a blood vessel due to restriction of blood supply) and transform into new blood vessel cells inside the heart muscle, also travelled in response to physical exercise. As we exercise, then, these stem cells replenish damaged blood vessel cells.

Such are the positive benefits of exercise for heart and blood vessel repair that at a meeting of the European Cardiology Society in August 2009, experts urged doctors to prescribe exercise over angioplasties, which are the insertion of stents to open the heart artery.

More exciting new evidence of the regenerative capacity of the heart comes from a 2009 study performed by scientists at the Karolinska Institute in Stockholm. The study made use of the fact that, prior to the banning of above-ground nuclear weapons testing in 1963, the testing produced radioactive carbon dioxide. Some of this, containing the form of carbon known as carbon-14, naturally found its way into the food chain, because plants absorb carbon dioxide to grow. As we eat the plants, the carbon-14 enters our body too and becomes part of our cellular and genetic structure. In this way, cells throughout the bodies of people born prior to 1963 have carbon-14 in them. There's no need to worry, though, if you were born before 1963 – carbon-14 is believed to be completely harmless.

The scientists at the Karolinska Institute monitored levels of carbon-14 in heart-muscle cells, known as cardiomyocytes. Surprisingly, they found that the levels were dropping as people got older. The heart-muscle cells, contrary to previous wisdom, were being renewed.

The scientists eventually discovered that cardiomyocytes renew at the rate of about 1 per cent per year at around age 25 and then gradually decline to around 0.45 per cent per year at around age 75.[15] To put this into perspective, it means that since a male heart contains about 4 billion heart-muscle cells, 40 million would be regenerating every year in our twenties and about 18 million would be regenerating a year in our seventies. That's a lot of cells, considering that the renewal of heart-muscle cells was previously thought to be impossible.

The percentages may sound small, but they are probably more than enough to repair much of the daily stress and lifestyle-related damage that the average person inflicts upon themselves. The scientists estimated that over half of an average person's heart cells might have been replaced by the time they reached the age of 50.

This discovery is a significant breakthrough, because if the heart is able to make new cells by itself then it's almost certain that there are ways of speeding up the process. This means that scar tissue following a heart attack can potentially be replaced with healthy tissue, something that has got many cardiologists very excited.

Some studies – for example the exercise studies mentioned earlier – suggest that the renewal of heart-muscle cells is through the transformation of stem cells. But other recent studies indicate that, although this is true, there might also be a second way in which they are renewed.

TURNING ON HEART-MUSCLE REGENERATION

As the body grows from a single cell into a body, cells divide. Two become four, four become eight, eight become sixteen, and so on. It was always thought that heart cells stopped dividing once they'd turned into fully formed adult heart-muscle cells. But a groundbreaking 2009 study overturned this assumption.

Studying mice, doctors in the Department of Cardiology at Boston Children's Hospital found that injecting a growth factor known as neuregulin1 (NRG1) prompted the cell division of heart-muscle cells, which eventually produced new and fully operational heart-muscle cells and also led to improved functioning of the heart after a heart attack. Contrary to what had always been thought, the heart can and *does* regenerate.[16]

In view of the results of a number of sociological studies, which will be discussed in the next chapter, it is highly likely that oxytocin plays a role in this process, both in the stem-cell conversion into heart-muscle cells and as a growth factor.

Many sociological studies show improved health and survival rates in those heart-attack patients who have good emotional and social support, who enjoy good-quality relationships or who have pets – all situations where oxytocin levels are high. The poorest health and survival rates are in those who are socially isolated or have poor-quality relationships – situations where oxytocin levels are low.

GROWING A HEART

Evidence of oxytocin's role in the conversion of stem cells into heart-muscle cells comes from recent research into the growth of heart-muscle cells in a foetus. The formation of cardiomyocytes in a growing foetus is known as cardiomyogenesis. The research, published in 2008 and led by scientists from the Department of Internal Medicine at the University of Cologne, Germany, found that oxytocin played a key role in this process.[17]

Stem cells can be imagined as flowers without a head. They are just stems. Imagine that each of these stems can grow any head so that it can morph into any one of numerous different types of flower. As it matures, it might grow a daffodil head and become a daffodil, or it might grow a rose head and become a rose. Similarly, a stem cell is an undefined cell that is just waiting to become a full cell of a particular type. It might become a heart cell, or a skin cell, or a liver or kidney cell.

In the study, when oxytocin was injected into partially formed heart-muscle cells that had evolved from embryonic stem cells, they started to beat: they had become fully formed, fully operational adult heart-muscle cells. It was concluded that oxytocin was encouraging the transformation and that it might also play a role in neurogenesis, which is the growth of brain cells.

The fact that oxytocin is involved in angiogenesis and can do some of what VEGF does may even mean that it is involved in the genesis of cells throughout the body. Research may well reveal this over the next few years.

In the absence of adequate amounts of oxytocin, the evidence seems to suggest that the transformation of stem cells into heart-muscle cells will be slower than normal. This is likely to be a reason why women who are abused when pregnant generally give birth to infants with lower than average birth weight. Abuse is associated with low oxytocin levels. These low levels will mean that the growth of the heart, and possibly the brain and other organs, will be slower than normal, resulting in a lower birth weight.[18] We should always look to show love, kindness and support to pregnant women.

In addition to oxytocin's crucial role in the growth of an infant heart, research might soon discover that it also plays a key role in the replenishment of heart-muscle cells from adult stem cells. As we'll discover in the next chapter, cardiac patients with the strongest interpersonal bonds and most fulfilling relationships have much less risk of a second heart attack and a greater life-expectancy than those with the weakest bonds. If heart-muscle cells are being regenerated from stem cells, and if this is actually repairing damage, as a growing body of researchers now believe, it seems that oxytocin has a part to play in the story.

It may even be revealed that it can do a similar job to NRG1 in the non-stem cell replenishment of heart muscle, just as it does a similar job to VEGF in the formation of new blood vessels. Thus it might be assisting heart regeneration on both fronts: transforming stem cells and encouraging the heart-muscle cells to re-enter the division process and renew themselves.

Given the extent of oxytocin's effects on the entire cardiovascular system, from binding to cells on blood vessels to dilate them and lower blood pressure to stimulating the growth of new blood vessels and encouraging the growth of a developing heart, it is almost certain that love, kindness, compassion and good-quality relationships indeed facilitate maximum health and regeneration of the heart.

Over dinner one night, my friend Ileen said, 'Isn't it amazing that when we do things from our hearts, we actually produce a chemical that is good for the heart?'

*****

The next chapter reveals some powerful scientific evidence for the impact of love, kindness, compassion and good-quality relationships on health and longevity, many of which are almost certainly facilitated by oxytocin – and hence kindness.

STORIES OF KINDNESS

A Wartime Memory

At one point during World War II, I got separated from my company. I was in a small town filled with bombed-out buildings. Some German soldiers were approaching and began searching the buildings. I was terrified. If they found me, they would kill me.

I tried my best to stay totally quiet. I was even scared to breathe in case anyone heard me. When the soldiers reached the building I was in, I was shaking with fear. I've never been so terrified in my life. I could hear someone really close. I grasped my gun, but I couldn't think straight.

Then he saw me. He was staring right at me with his gun raised. I didn't raise mine – I was too scared. Then I lost control and wet myself, right there in front of him.

He looked at me for a moment, then he took me by surprise. He squinted his eyes a little, then gave me a compassionate smile and a gentle nod and walked away, signalling to the other soldiers that the building was clear.

I've never forgotten that. It's the thing I most remember about the war. **Jack**

CHAPTER 9

SUPPORTING THE HEART

'As the seat of our deepest feelings, the heart is, as we know, all too sensitive, registering through pains, pangs, flutters and skips the thousand varieties of suffering that Buddhists claim humans experience – from anger, jealousy and fear to terror, shame, and all too often, sadness.'

Dr Mimi Guarneri, from *The Heart Speaks*

Ever heard of the Roseto effect? Roseto is a town in Pennsylvania, USA, whose inhabitants participated in a scientific study lasting almost 50 years. Despite their lifestyle, which was similar to most of the rest of the USA at the time (not the healthiest in the world!), the rate of death by heart disease in Roseto was half the national average for men aged over 65 and almost zero for men aged 55–64.

It turned out that what protected them from heart disease was each other. Love and a sense of connection, it seemed, over-ruled diet as far as the heart was concerned. The people of Roseto lived, ate, drank and worked together as a unit. Neigh-bours helped each other. The elders knew the middle names of every child on the street. In many households, there were over four generations of family living together. Regular social gather-ings also brought the whole community together.

Communities in most towns and cities don't share as much as they did in Roseto, nor do they have the same sense of together-ness. Even in Roseto, as society evolved, the residents became more isolated from each other. Many of the later generations took up opportunities that their parents had created for them and moved away. Many learned to look out for themselves and, in turn, became more isolated from their communities. Gradually, the shared sense of togetherness and purpose was lost and with it went protection from heart disease.

The result was that 1970 saw the first ever death from a heart attack of an under-45-year-old in Roseto. Nowadays the death rate from heart attacks is pretty much the same there as any-where else in the USA, as the sense of community in Roseto is now the same as it is throughout the rest of the country.[1]

When a cultural identity keeps people together in a community that is interconnected and where their daily lives involve kind-ness towards each other, they are largely protected against heart disease.

A seven-year study of men of Japanese ancestry now living in Hawaii found the same thing. The scientists concluded that their interconnectedness – their social networks, relationships and sense of community – protected them from heart disease.[2]

The heart is a remarkable organ that it is acutely sensitive to our lifestyle and our emotions. It's so sensitive that diseases of the heart are the leading cause of death in the western world. According to a 2008 report, heart disease accounts for 198,000 deaths in the UK every year: one in three of all deaths.[3] And genetics play only a small role in heart disease.

With the new evidence of the protective effects of oxytocin on the heart, many of these deaths can now be prevented. Not only should those at risk make lifestyle changes like taking exercise and eating a better diet, but they should also work on the quality of their relationships by trying to bring more love and kindness into their lives.

Many of us can be the *source* of more love and kindness in our lives by giving it to others. As Gandhi said, 'We must be the change we wish to see.' We should not wait for others to come to us; we should go to them. We can individually start the love, kindness and compassion ball rolling in our lives. And good relationships will spontaneously arise from the fire we build.

The heart yearns for love. We know this intuitively. This is why we associate love with the heart. It knows that the best love comes from contact with other people and so we yearn for closeness with others. Scientific evidence now clearly shows that when we have it we are at our healthiest and happiest.

Being socially isolated from others is not so good for us. Although many people want to be by themselves, which is a symptom of the daily stresses we are often under and the consequent need for escape, having friends or loved ones to share things with is good for the heart. In fact, it is crucial for the heart. Some studies show that social isolation increases the risk of heart disease by two to three times.

A study of 149 angina patients, for instance, found that those who reported the most love and support in their lives had the lowest amounts of coronary artery disease.[4]

At the Scripps Center for Integrative Medicine, cardiologist Dr Mimi Guarneri writes that cardiac patients benefit more from counselling and support groups, situations that produce oxytocin, than from the vegetarian meals they receive, or the meditation or yoga that they participate in.[5] Sharing our stories and our thoughts with others is so important to us because it helps us to bond with each other. That need is wired into our nervous system. As we shall learn in a later chapter, we are genetically wired to be together. This is why isolation eventually leads to ill health for most.

Our modern way of life actually creates separation. We share less as we all strive to have our own stuff. We use computers to send e-mail to someone a few corridors away, depriving our hearts of that much-needed connection. We believe that e-mail helps us get more done. But the quality of communication is better when we connect face to face.

In my final year in the pharmaceutical industry, I chose to stop using e-mail to ask questions and get things done and started knocking on doors. My productivity soared. I ended up managing 11 active projects compared to an average of four throughout the rest of the team. People are more inclined to help when you connect with them.

GET CONNECTED

The scientists involved in the Roseto study concluded that a sense of social interconnectedness was a better predictor of a healthy heart than smoking or cholesterol. We now know this to be true from a number of other studies. Hostility and stress, for instance, things that separate us from others, are more influential in the development of heart disease than a poor diet or lack of exercise. A hostile, cynical or aggressive attitude is known to increase levels of interleukin-6, which is indicative of inflammation.

A 1992 study found that living alone was a risk factor for a subsequent heart attack if a patient had already had one.[6] Examining 1,497 patients for a period of one to four years, the scientists found that 15.8 per cent of those living alone had another heart attack within six months of the first one, compared with only 8.8 per cent of those who were not living alone. Living with someone reduced the chances of a further heart attack by almost half. If you know someone who may be lonely, especially an elderly person or someone new to your neighbourhood, why not show kindness and visit them?

A 2005 study published in the journal *Psychosomatic Medicine* also found that small social networks (defined as 'number of people in the household, marital status') were associated with higher levels of coronary artery calcification.[7] Examining the health of 783 participants, scientists from the Uniformed Services University of Health Sciences, Bethesda, in the USA, discovered that those with the smallest social networks and who were single or widowed had the greatest incidences of coronary artery calcification. Although the scientists did not consider the full network of friends and acquaintances, the study clearly showed that being isolated was linked with hardening of the arteries.

A large number of studies now clearly show that people who are socially involved have lower death rates than those who are socially isolated. In a 1979 study, people with few social ties had a two to three times greater mortality rate than those with more social ties.[8] In a 1987 study of 17,000 Swedish people, those who were socially involved had a four times lower death rate.[9]

In a 30-year study of 427 wives and mothers, those who had multiple roles, which included volunteering at least once a week, were found to live longest. The scientists concluded that the social contact created through the multiple roles was one of the main factors that prolonged their lives.[10]

There is even evidence that having social support even offers some protection against arthritis and even TB.[11]

As research into oxytocin shows that it protects against heart disease, it seems increasingly likely that it plays a role in the protective effect of social contact. We know, for instance, that oxytocin offers protection against atherosclerosis. So does social contact. It is highly likely that oxytocin was flowing like a river through the arteries of the residents of Roseto.

And one of the characteristics of social contact is kindness. We look out for our friends and family. We show that we care by helping them through difficult times as we share in the highs and lows of each other's lives. Kindness plays a key role in the protective effects of social contact.

HAPPY MARRIAGE, HAPPY HEART

Several studies have shown that people in marriages live longer than single people, enjoying better protection from heart disease and even cancer.

In the National Longitudinal Mortality Study (NLMS) in the USA, conducted by the US Bureau of the Census and published in 2000, for instance, the marital status of 281,460 men and women aged 45 years and older was compared with mortality. The scientists found that unmarried persons aged 45–64 had a significantly higher risk of mortality than married persons. The risk for older married couples was still increased, but less so. When they examined mortality for only cardiovascular disease, unmarried people were also significantly more at risk than married people. And the risk factor for people who were widowed, divorced or separated was much higher than it was for single people.[12]

A similar effect was found in the British Regional Heart Study published in 1995. The study involved 7,735 men aged 40–59 whose marital status and mortality were assessed over a period of 11.5 years. The study found that being single was associated with an increased risk of death from cardiovascular disease.[13]

Growing evidence now suggests, however, that it's not marriage itself that is health-enhancing, but the quality of the relationship.[14] For instance, compared with a happy marriage, a 1986 study found that an unhappy marriage was associated with a 25-fold increase in major depression.[15] And a 1994 study involving 328 married couples also found that an unhappy marriage was linked to depression, citing a 10 times greater likelihood that people in unhappy marriages would suffer depression within 18–30 months of getting married.[16]

The prognosis for unhappy marriages is not so good for cardiac health either. A 2000 study of 292 female patients who were in hospital with either a heart attack or unstable angina found that those who had high levels of marital stress were 2.9 times more likely to suffer another coronary event, which included another heart attack or death. Specifically, the scientists who conducted the study made it very clear that it was marital stress and not work stress that damaged the heart.[17]

Similarly, a 2001 study of 189 patients with congestive heart failure (139 men and 50 women) and their spouses found that the quality of marriage was linked to the likelihood of surviving the next four years. Better quality of marriage equalled better chance of survival.[18]

A 2006 study, following up on the same patients four years later, found that the quality of their marriage continued to be associated with their quality of health. Those in better-quality marriages were in better health than those whose relationship quality was poor.[19]

A 2004 study even found that stable partnerships were associated with a slower rate of progress of HIV to AIDS in patients who were receiving HAART (highly active antiretroviral therapy).[20]

A 2005 study showed that marital quality was also linked with the prevalence of metabolic syndrome. (Metabolic syndrome is a cluster of medical disorders that often includes increased blood pressure, increased insulin levels, high cholesterol and excess fat around the waist and that increases a person's risk of heart disease, stroke and diabetes.) The study, performed by scientists at Pittsburgh University, examined 413 middle-aged women and discovered that those who were dissatisfied with their marriage or even widowed were more likely to have metabolic syndrome than those in happy marriages.[21]

Some scientists can now determine the quality of marital relationships by the language of the heart patient and the spouse. In a 2008 study carried out by scientists from the University of Arizona, 57 heart-failure patients and their spouses were recorded as they talked about how they coped with the heart problem. When they analysed the language use afterwards, the scientists found that those whose symptoms improved the most over the following six months were the ones whose spouses used the word 'we' the most. The spouses clearly considered themselves and their heart-patient partner a unit, a team, and this protected them to some extent. The use of the word 'we' suggested a stronger bond between them.[22]

Conversely, when there's more 'I' talk, it can indicate that the relationship is of poorer quality. There is a greater sense of separateness, of isolation. The use of the word 'we' is suggestive of a stronger bond. And with this stronger bond, there are no doubt greater amounts of oxytocin, which will help in the recovery process.

In her excellent book *The Heart Speaks*, Dr Mimi Guarneri mentions an old saying: 'The *I* in illness is isolation, and the crucial letters in wellness are *we*.' Scientific evidence is now showing us just how true this wisdom is.

Hostility is one of the strongest predictors of heart disease. Several studies have now shown that measuring hostility levels in people is one of the most reliable ways to predict a person's risk of heart disease, as reliable as having information on diet and exercise.[23]

In a marriage, hostile interactions between a couple increase blood pressure, weaken the immune system, slow wound healing, increase levels of several pro-inflammatory cytokines, increase stress hormone levels and have been linked with coronary artery calcification and other forms of heart disease. A 2006 study, for instance, showed that hostility and cynicism were related to high levels of interleukin-6.[24]

Making an effort to communicate supportively, despite how difficult it can be, to listen and to try to understand the other's perspective has positive consequences. In a 2006 study led by Janice Kiecolt-Glaser of Ohio State University, 90 newly wed couples were studied during a 30-minute conflict task. Stress hormone levels rose as hostility increased; however, when the couples were supportive of each other and constructively engaged in discussions, stress hormone levels declined.[25]

In another study, people labelled as hostile and who had chest pain were asked, as part of the study, to clean each other's laundry. This simple act led to much less chest pain.[26] It's funny how doing someone's washing can do the same as a heart drug. Thoughts of kindness replace thoughts of hostility and oxytocin flows through the heart.

Intimacy has been shown to buffer the effects of stress, which will therefore have protective effects on the heart. In a 2008 study, 51 couples reported how much time they spent on intimacy and gave saliva samples, from which the stress hormone cortisol was measured, every three hours for one week. Those couples who spent the most time in intimacy had significantly lower levels of cortisol than couples who had low levels of intimacy. The scientists also noted that, despite some stress at work, the intimacy was a buffer on cortisol increases. It neutralized them. Those couples who were less intimate had higher levels of cortisol during work stress.[27]

There is so much that can be done to heal difficult relationships and the healing can make a huge difference to health. For some, it can be a matter of life or death. Love and kindness are so crucial to the heart. Rather than running off to the divorce courts, it may be worthwhile checking out some options that can change how you feel about your partner. I have listed a few below, for the sake of good health.

FOUR SUGGESTIONS FOR HEALING BROKEN RELATIONSHIPS AND THE HEART

1. Try to talk to each other. If there are serious problems then honesty might just be the solution that can give you a place to start from. If this is difficult then perhaps mediation may help. There are plenty of experts in the field of mediation.

2. Based on the evidence cited throughout this book, I would also suggest trying a gratitude journal. You may be surprised how making a list of five to ten things a day that you are grateful for can relieve stress and depression and give you a more positive outlook. Sometimes, stress or depression can block your vision of your partner and cause you to forget many of the reasons you fell for them in the first place. Gratitude, as we shall learn in a later chapter, will help you to see all that is good. In particular, keep a journal of all that you are grateful for about your partner. Include all that they have contributed to your life, from happiness to life circumstances, even to material things. Don't hold back. People can have significant breakthroughs doing this exercise, realizing that they have taken their partner for granted for a long time.

3. Despite your challenges with your partner, you could try kindness. Sometimes making an effort to do kind things for your partner can tap into a feeling of deep love and caring for them. For some, this can rekindle relationships.

4. If you find it difficult to stop picking fault with your partner, which really does neither of you any good, try using a 'complaint-free' wristband or bracelet. This is an idea that was put forward by Will Bowen in his book *A Complaint-Free World*. Each time you find yourself getting on at your partner, criticizing them or judging them, you have to change the wristband to your other wrist. The challenge is to go a full 21 days without complaining about someone or criticizing, picking on or judging them. Each time you change the wristband to the other wrist you have to go back to day 1. It's only 21 days. Do you feel that your relationship deserves that chance?

GET GOOD AT BEING FRIENDS

Regardless of whether we're in stable relationships or not, having friends who can offer you emotional support, which is a show of kindness, and vice versa, is health-giving. It is cardioprotective. The more emotional support people have, the less chance they have of becoming seriously ill, especially from heart disease.

A 1994 study of 391 men and 377 women, for instance, found that those who had the greatest emotional social support had the lowest levels of stress hormones in urine samples. Those who had least emotional support had highest stress hormone levels.[28]

Some research has shown that social ties need to involve some feelings of intimacy and belonging to have the health-giving effects.[29] Those times when we truly bond with a friend, as we get to know the real person, as we help them or they help us get through a difficult time, are good for us. Having emotional social support activates the parasympathetic branch of the autonomic nervous system, which is the 'rest and relax' part that sends the body into a healthy, relaxed and regenerative mode. A lack of intimate contact, on the other hand, is associated with greater activation of the sympathetic branch, the 'fight or flight', which is linked with heart disease if too active for too long.[30]

Some evidence is now suggesting, of course, that some of the beneficial effects of emotional social support come from oxytocin.[31]

The following is a simple but powerful exercise that can help you to improve your connectedness with others.

IMPROVING YOUR RELATIONSHIPS AND CONNECTEDNESS

Take a piece of paper and draw a line down the centre of the page, or open a journal at a double blank page.

On the left-hand side, write about your relationships with others and your sense of connection with them. Give each a score on a scale of 0 to 10, where zero is no connection and 10 is a beautiful, fulfilling connection. Include your loved ones and friends in the list and then go on to people you work with or just see occasionally.

On the right-hand side, write about how you can improve upon these relationships. Be honest with yourself and describe the changes you'd like to see. Also make some notes about how you intend to go about making these improvements, not in the other person(s) but in yourself. Write what *you* intend to think, say and do differently.

Be sure to act on your own recommendations.

So we need relationships to have healthy hearts. Despite the evidence that a bad diet is unhealthy, a sense of togetherness with a rich network of people might even trump its negative effects. Of course, that's no reason to eat unhealthily!

Still, the quality of our relationships is far more important to our health than we ever thought. Marriage is good for the heart, but only if it is a good-quality relationship. If the quality is poor then it can be worse for the heart than living in social isolation. We know that the heart needs love. So, as long as we remain kind and compassionate to those around us, our relationships should stay strong and we should stay healthy.

STORIES OF KINDNESS

Help with our Sofa

We were moving house a few months ago. We didn't have far to go, as we were only moving to the other end of the apartment complex that we were living in. But after filling our car with boxes and stuff for about the tenth time, driving it 200 yards down the road, emptying it and carrying all the stuff up a flight of stairs, we realized that it had been a mistake not to hire a removals company, or at least a van.

Although it was tiring, we got to around 5 p.m., having started at 7.30 a.m., with only our two sofas to go. The day before, we'd thought we could easily carry them down the road. Now it didn't seem such a good idea.

So there we were, carrying the first sofa and stopping every 10 yards for a rest. It was especially hard for my partner, Elizabeth, as she is half my size. We'd got about 50 yards when a man who was walking along the road stopped, introduced himself as Tony and offered some help. It turned out that he was one of our neighbours in the complex. So Tony and I carried the sofa down the rest of the road. It might not have seemed like much to him, but it made a huge difference to us.

But we were only half done. We still had another sofa, albeit a smaller two-seater, to take to the new apartment. So about 15 minutes later, it was déjà vu as we were carrying it down the road and stopping every 10 yards or so for a short rest.

This time we'd got about 80 yards down the road when a white van stopped and two Polish men jumped out. They didn't speak any English but just gave a few nods and friendly gestures as they picked up the sofa. We all carried it down the road, exchanging nods and smiles. Elizabeth held open the doors as we squeezed the sofa around corners and up the stairs. The Polish men carried it all the way into the lounge, with not a word spoken. When they placed it down they just smiled and nodded a few times and walked out of the door.

CHAPTER 10

WHY BABIES NEED LOVE

**'A baby is born with a need to be loved –
and never grows out of it.'**
Frank A. Clark

We have seen so far that adults need love and kindness, but what about infants? They have to grow within the environment that we create for them. What if we create one infused with kindness? When then?

The emotional environment – the love, care and attention an infant receives from its parents – plays a hugely important role in the development of its brain. Just as a flower won't fully grow if it doesn't have the sun, so a brain won't fully grow if it doesn't have positive experiences. The basic scaffolding of the neural circuits of the brain of a foetus are built in the womb following the genetic programme inherited from the parents. The experiences of the infant in the few years after it is born, however, build upon and shape those circuits.[1]

The primary caregiver – the parent or person who spends most time with a baby – therefore has a huge influence on the brain's neural circuits. Their love, care, play and responsiveness build and enhance the circuits required for the infant to function well in the world in later years. When they are emotionally responsive and in tune with the needs of the infant, showing love, care, attention and joy, the results are positive. However, they can have a significantly detrimental effect on the growth of the infant's brain if their behaviour towards it is mostly negative or unresponsive to its needs.

There's much more to 'formula', then, than milk and food. The best formula contains love, care, play, joy and responsiveness to ensure the growth of the infant brain.

HOW THE BRAIN GROWS

After birth, the brain grows fast. There's a huge increase in the volume and complexity of the wiring, which is the number of brain cells (neurons) and neural connections (the wires between the neurons) being forged. It is especially fast between the ages of 6 and 12 months and in the prefrontal cortex, the area above the eyes that gives us the capacity to reason and make choices.[2]

Think of it like a forest, as we did in an earlier chapter. The forest is sparse in the beginning, with some branches reaching out and touching the branches of neighbouring trees. Now imagine that many, many new seeds are being sown every day. New trees begin to grow to occupy more of the space in the forest and they also grow branches that touch other trees. Soon the forest is dense and expanding. In the brain, the trees are neurons and the branches that connect them are neural connections.

But the forest needs food to grow. In the brain, a lot of the nourishment comes from the love of the parents or primary caregiver.

It's like fertilizer. In chemical terms, beta-endorphin, which is a neuropeptide that gives us pleasure, is released into the baby's brain and body. In the brain, it travels to the orbitofrontal cortex, the part of the prefrontal cortex behind the orbits of the eyes, and helps neurons to grow there. At the same time, dopamine is released from the brainstem and also makes its way to the prefrontal cortex, also helping its growth.

And with this plentiful supply of dopamine come more benefits. Dopamine is involved in the positive processing of experiences. When it flows, the growing child is more positive in how it approaches situations and adapts to things and people quickly. This happens readily when the parent shows happiness or joy, or positively interacts with the infant in any way. Thus, at the biological level, a parent's joy and the love, kindness and attention they show as they interact with their child encourage the growth of its brain.

And as the brain grows, cells speak to other cells via the neural connections to coordinate the functioning of the body – breathing, digestion, movement and other bodily functions. Biologically, neural connections are fibres of protein that connect one neuron to another, allowing information to pass throughout the network. The influence of the environment is important because of the way it affects the connections. Studies show that the more positive experiences an infant has, the more neural connections are created and the better that information is passed throughout the brain. Too many negative or stressful experiences burn many of them out, especially in the frontal cortex.

As a child grows, the number of neurons and neural connections eventually becomes much more than is needed and a process known as 'neural pruning' takes place. The number of neurons and connections is 'pruned' back, just as an overgrown hedge can be pruned back to a healthy size. The overall number of brain cells therefore reduces to approximately the number we have as adults. This pruning process is mostly the result of the life experience of the child. Less pruning takes place if a child's environment has been positive than if it has been full of neglect and stress. It's a case of 'use it or lose it', just like a muscle. Connections not used are pruned back. Those used are retained. Thus, for many people, the number of neurons they have, the richness of their neural network and the complexity of their wiring reflect their quality of life in the early years. Love, kindness and strong bonds equal rich, developed neural circuits and a healthy brain.

When children are institutionalized, it is believed to cause overkill, so to speak. Through lack of use due to lack of positive stimulation and positive emotional environment, many more neurons and neural connections are pruned back than in children from stable homes, leading to a less richly wired, underpowered brain. Having an underpowered brain, of course, has its consequences, which many studies have revealed. Among them are slower growth and thus smaller body size, reduced brain activity and more emotional problems, which include depression, stress, antisocial behaviour and difficulty fitting in.

One of the consequences of having a well-developed prefrontal cortex through early experience, on the other hand, is that depression is less likely in adulthood. Such children grow up to be well-rounded individuals who fit in and are emotionally equipped to deal with the trials and tribulations of life. Adults with a well-developed prefrontal cortex also have greater self-control, self-compassion and a greater sense of connection with others. These are the gifts that we can give our children by loving them and taking the time to respond to their needs.

WHEN YOU'RE HAPPY, YOUR BABY IS HAPPY TOO

And babies are more aware of their parents' behaviour than you might think. The human brain is wired to pick up on facial expressions and even pupil size from birth. The process is, of course, not conscious – the ability is genetic. But even though babies can't consciously discriminate between what is happy behaviour and what is sad behaviour, the brain reacts differently to both.

As adults, we detect subtle millisecond flashes of emotion in each other's eyes and faces, as we learned in an earlier chapter. This is why we sometimes just get a 'feeling' about someone. It is part of the intuition equation. This way we are able to empathize with people, to understand them by partially sharing their emotions.

Babies are adept at it too. This is how they read their parents' emotional state. They can pick up on the size of the pupils and the facial expressions of their parents and this is translated in their brain. Dilated pupils, for instance, inform the baby's brain that the parent is happy. Through the empathy circuit, this then inspires happiness in the baby too by releasing happy chemicals in the brain. Studies show that it also activates the left frontal region of the brain. Sadness, as you would expect, has the opposite effect, activating the right frontal region.[3]

EARLY EXPERIENCE

An area of the brain that is particularly affected by early environment is the orbitofrontal cortex, which sits in the frontal lobes, just above the orbits of the eyes, hence its name within the frontal cortex. This grows mostly after birth and begins to mature from around the age of one, growing almost in entirety within the environment created by the parents. It is believed to be involved in decision-making and helps us to reason without having an emotional knee-jerk reaction. As children, and later as adults, it gives us the ability to think before we react to things, when someone offends us, for instance. It is thought that it also helps us to understand personal and social boundaries. People with damaged or impaired orbitofrontal cortices are usually socially dysfunctional.

Without proper development in this part of the brain, children and adults react to negative or challenging situations without thinking, or at least without any conscious control over their responses. The richer the growth there, the more self-control they have.

WHEN EARLY EXPERIENCE IS NEGATIVE

A large number of studies clearly show that if an infant is deprived of love, care or attention, its brain does not fully develop. Holes appear in the forest of neurons and this limits the power of the brain and the capacity of the child to function in the world.

The areas most heavily affected by love deprivation include the prefrontal cortex and the orbitofrontal cortex within it. This is especially clear in studies of institutionalized children.

One study, conducted by doctors at Wayne State University, used PET scans to examine the brains of ten children (six boys and four girls) of an average age of nine from Romanian orphanages. Compared with the brains of children in control groups, who had been raised in normal homes, the Romanian orphans had greatly reduced activity in several brain regions, including the orbitofrontal cortex, areas involved in higher cognition, emotion and emotion regulation.[4]

Other studies of institutionalized children show delays in social and emotional development as well as the development of aggressive behaviour, inattention, hyperactivity and even symptoms similar to autism, all of which are a result of an underdeveloped brain.

A large study known as the Bucharest Early Intervention Project (BEIP) found that children in institutions fall behind in overall physical as well as emotional development.[5] Their body (bones, muscles, etc.), internal organs and brain fail to grow as they should, a condition referred to as psychosocial dwarfism, or non-organic failure to thrive. Their heights and weights are almost always below average for their age. The effect is considerable. Infants in orphanages around the world fall behind one month in growth for every two to three months in an orphanage.

Please don't underestimate this – it is massive! Because of the impact on the growth of the brain, withdrawal, emotional problems and even behavioural problems are the natural consequences when these children grow up, in addition to their small size and poorer health.

A 2009 study conducted by scientists from Harvard University examined the impact of institutionalized care on memory and executive function – the capacity to plan and make decisions – which is governed by the prefrontal cortex in the brain. When assessed at eight years of age and compared with children who had been reared in normal homes, those children with a history of institutionalized care (part of the BEIP) were found to have much poorer memories and weaker executive functions than children who hadn't spent time in institutions.[6]

BUT THERE IS HOPE

Many studies now show that adoption or foster care offers some hope for institutionalized children.

A 2009 study, conducted by psychologists at St John Fisher College, Rochester, USA, examined the impact of foster care on children's attention and ability to emotionally express themselves. They found that at both 30 months and 42 months of age, children who were fostered had much higher levels of attention and expressed much more positive emotion than children who remained in institutions.[7]

A 2007 meta-analysis of 33 scientific papers covering 122 studies examined the impact of international adoption of institutionalized children and clearly showed that the more time children spent in institutions, the more their growth was affected. Longer residents were smaller in height, weighed less and even had smaller head circumference. At the time they were adopted, most of the children were lagging behind children reared in normal homes.[8]

However the analysis found that after adoption most of the children almost completely caught up in height and weight. The title of the meta-analysis even contained the words 'evidence of massive catch-up after international adoption', although the scientists did find that the rate of catch-up of head circumference was slower than it was for height and weight, which they suggested was linked with brain development.

Another outcome they found was that the later the children were adopted, the more slowly they caught up. But hope clearly lies in adopting children or even fostering them.

This is what the Bucharest Early Intervention Project also found. It included 136 children in Romanian institutions, aged between 6 months and 31 months. Sixty-eight of them remained in the institutions and the other 68 were assigned to foster care, where they were placed into 56 diverse families. The project compared them with 72 normal children who had never been placed in institutions.

The results were dramatic. Many children, when taken into foster care where they were loved and cared for on a personal level, began to grow at a normal rate, gaining height and weight. They also became more attentive, and even their IQ scores increased. And, importantly, they also had much more positive emotion in their lives.

But, just as the 2007 meta-analysis found, the study also found that it was important to get in there early. The true benefits only took root if the children were taken into foster care before they reached two years of age. Beyond that, foster care didn't have as much of an impact.[9]

Many of the brain's circuits that are related to emotional development are laid down by two years of age. This means that the brain gets used to having a certain number of neurons and neural connections and these get used to acting at a certain power level. Indeed, when the scientists studied the EEG results, it became clear that the children taken into foster care before the age of two showed much greater brain activity over their whole brain than those taken into care after the age of two.

A 2007 Harvard study found the same thing. Children from institutions placed into foster care early showed greater mental and emotional improvement than children who were fostered later.[10]

The emotional improvements in children who are adopted or taken into foster care give them a better chance of a fulfilling life when they grow up. So it is important to 'rescue' infants at an early age. However, it's also important to realize that even if a child hasn't experienced a loving environment this does *not* automatically mean that it will have emotional problems as it grows up, even if it has been reared for a long time in an institution, only that it might be harder work for the parents. Studies don't take this into account when quoting results – they just examine the average results over a number of children and families. When there are difficulties, extra care, support and attentiveness can

save the day. Many skilled foster and adoptive parents have suc-
ceeded in transforming troubled children into caring adults with
huge hearts who go on to have loving relationships and raise
emotionally balanced children themselves. Early damage can be
repaired through excellent parenting.

What about places where the infrastructure doesn't yet exist
for foster care? If children must be kept in institutions, evidence
shows that small family-like group settings in the institutions are
better for them.

Institutions and orphaned children are widespread in central and
eastern Europe. In 2004, UNICEF estimated that there were
approximately 1.5 million children living in orphanages, psychiatric units and group homes.[11] But it's not just in Europe where
the problem lies. It's much worse in other parts of the world. In
2006, there were over 100 million children living without available
caregivers. In Asia, there were 65 million. In Africa, 34 million. In
Latin America and the Caribbean, 8 million.[12]

Adoption and fostering can rescue some of the infants in institutions, not just in the sense of giving them a home, but in saving
them from the negative health consequences of institutionalized
life.

It takes great courage, patience and, of course, a large heart to
foster or adopt a child. But the love is well placed, for it gives
a chance to a child who otherwise may never get one. I have
noticed a lot of judgement in the media of celebrities adopting
children from poor countries. We should trust that the celebrities
choose to adopt because they, just like we, care and want to give
a child a better chance in life.

Judgement gets in the way of our natural tenderness, our natural
kindness. Sophocles wrote, 'Men of ill judgement often ignore

the good that lies within their hands, till they have lost it,' and Mother Teresa said, 'If you judge people, you have no time to love them.'

When we judge others, we separate ourselves from our natural tendency to care and be kind. And when we do, we may just get in the way of the best chance a child might ever get.

THE POWER OF A KIND HAND

Part of a positive emotional environment involves touch. All of us need warm touch. Why is it important? We know that positive person-to-person contact produces oxytocin in the brain and body. Without adequate contact from a positive and loving early environment, a child's brain might not have the benefits of oxytocin to dampen some of the anxiety and fear from the amygdala, causing it to interpret many circumstances in life in a threatening way.

Institutionalization, of course, also affects oxytocin levels. A 2005 study performed by scientists at the University of Wisconsin indeed found that children who had been institutionalized had much lower levels of oxytocin than normal children after interacting with their caregiver.[13]

In the study, children from Romanian orphanages who had been adopted by American families at 18 months of age were compared with 18-month-old children raised in stable American homes. When the children played with their mother, oxytocin levels increased in the typical American children, as we would expect, but they did not rise in the children who had spent their time since birth in an orphanage.

Warm touch is undoubtedly a part of the experiences of adopted and fostered children and will account for part of the accelerated growth enjoyed by orphans who are adopted or fostered. But these types of results don't just relate to institutions. Positive emotional deprivation and touch deprivation produce many of the same effects. The brains of all children need positive emotion and warm touch to wire correctly.

Touch goes beyond producing oxytocin, however. Positive touch is essential to stimulate growth in the body. A 2008 report even showed that warm touch, in the form of massage, could stimulate the vagus nerve, which improved weight gain by stimulating gastric motility. It also improved the positive emotional experience of the infant and the authors of the report even suggested that it might improve the social behaviour of children with autism, who have been noted to have low vagal tone. The study also pointed out that vagal tone improved during positive parent-infant interaction and thus interactions fused with love and kindness would improve the rate of growth of infants.[14]

Genetics research shows that warm touch activates a number of genes, including those required for growth. Adequate levels of warm contact, then, might be just the tonic when very young infants are in need of growth.

Warm touch also might explain the following profound recovery of a sick baby.

MIRACLE IN MASSACHUSETTS
On 17 October 1995, twins Kyrie and Brielle Jackson were born 12 weeks premature in Worcester, Massachusetts, Boston, weighing in at around two pounds each. Over the next few days, Kyrie gained weight but Brielle struggled. Sometimes she would cry and cry until she was gasping for breath so much that her face turned blue.

On one really bad day for Brielle in the Neonatal ICU, 19-year old nurse Gayle Kasparian was trying everything to settle her but nothing was working. Brielle was in a really bad state.

But then nurse Kasparian had an idea. With the permission of the parents, she took Kyrie out of her incubator and placed her into Brielle's incubator, something that was against the hospital's standard practice. Separate incubators were always used to reduce the risk of cross-infection.

Then a miracle happened. As doctors and nurses watched, little Kyrie moved her arm and placed it around Brielle, apparently hugging her tiny sister. Almost immediately, Brielle began to get stronger. Her heart rate stabilized, her temperature returned to normal, her very low blood oxygen saturation levels rose rapidly and she started breathing much better, in synch with Kyrie, her blue colour becoming a healthy pink. Over the next few days, both twins grew stronger.

The hospital later changed its policy.

SOME LATER CONSEQUENCES OF AN UNDERDEVELOPED BRAIN

Another consequence of an infant or young child being starved of good amounts of love and affection is that it can cause behavioural problems as they grow up. With less neurological capacity to stop to think before acting, through an underdeveloped prefrontal cortex, children, teenagers and adults are more at risk of becoming antisocial and even indulging in criminal behaviour.

In a sense, some people who commit acts or robbery or violence might be invisibly handicapped. The prefrontal cortex allows us to step back, consider things for a moment and choose the most mature, or evolved, course of action. People who lack an adequate structure in the prefrontal cortex are at a significant social disadvantage. When a situation arises that requires restraint, they may have less ability to restrain themselves than someone who grew up in a different environment.

It does little good to punish parents for their children's behaviour. Often, the parents themselves have not learned how to behave maturely, nor have they the neural wiring in the prefrontal cortex necessary to have any positive experience in managing their emotions.

I was with Elizabeth's dad, Peter, in a small town once when a teen mum raising an angry voice at her toddler caught our attention. Peter turned to me and compassionately said, 'Poor thing. It's got no chance.' I had to agree. Quietly to myself, I also felt a pang of sympathy for the mum. If this snapshot of behaviour was normal for her, it was likely she had never learned a more mature way to behave. She may have had a poorly developed prefrontal cortex, a legacy of her own upbringing.

All of us, as a society, should bear responsibility for this. I think that on the one hand we have been too quick to blame parents for not controlling their children and on the other hand we have been too quick to blame genetics. What we've missed is that the *early environment* is absolutely crucial and that this is when many parents most need help. If a baby has grown in an environment of frequent bursts of anger or rage, attempts to discipline it as a teenager might be fruitless.

Therefore we should be more compassionate towards the behaviour of others. It does little good for peace and harmony in the world if we pass judgement on them without understanding the circumstances of their life leading up to their acts. 'Seek first to understand,' wrote St Francis of Assisi.

In the UK, prisons are bursting at the seams and I have repeatedly heard government ministers declare that they will 'get tough on crime'. This is not meant as a criticism, since many government policies are built out of what ministers think people want to see. But consider some of the research into the neural state of murderers. A 1997 study performed by scientists at the University of Southern California and Mount Sinai School of Medicine, New York, compared the brains of 41 murderers who had pleaded not guilty by reason of insanity with the brains of 41 controls. Not surprisingly, they found that the murderers had much lower activity in the prefrontal cortex region. They also had abnormal imbalances between their left and right prefrontal cortices and left and right orbitofrontal cortices, with the left being less developed than the right. This suggests much less self-control and fewer positive emotions, even less ability to feel positive emotions and more ability to feel negative emotions, like fear and anger for instance.

The authors of the study wrote, of the prefrontal cortex, 'Damage to this brain region can result in impulsivity, loss of self-control, immaturity, altered emotionality, and the inability to modify behaviour, which can in turn facilitate aggressive acts.'[15]

There were also abnormalities in the hippocampus and the amygdala. Together with the prefrontal cortex, these regions make up some of the emotional architecture of the brain and affect how we regulate and control our emotions. With less activity there, individuals have less ability at the neural level to control their emotions. As we all know, as we all have difficulties with our emotions at times, this can be a huge hindrance.

What we miss when we get tough on crime is empathy. This is not to excuse violence, but only to say that some people are neurologically wired, through no fault of their own, to have violent tendencies. We need to share the pain of the victims of crime while at the same time move towards an understanding of the perpetrators.

I'm hopeful that we can use some of this research to set out on a journey towards understanding. We will not create a better world by locking up every offender, but by trying to understand them, and then, as the Buddhist loving-kindness meditation teaches us, developing compassion for them. This, I am convinced, would make more of a contribution to peace and happiness in the world than getting tough on crime.

I'm not suggesting that we let everyone off, only that we try to understand and to practise compassion. Understanding breeds empathy, and this breeds compassion, which ultimately breeds forgiveness and kindness. And from there we can responsibly take steps towards helping to rehabilitate offenders. How else can we create a mature world?

In her excellent book, *Why Love Matters*, which I would recommend to all parents, Sue Gerhardt writes,

'If you meet a teenage mugger on the street one night, the last thing that you will be thinking about is his infancy. But the fear and rage evoked in you are probably the same feelings that have been with him since babyhood, which have been instrumental in transforming this particular baby into an antisocial thug.'[16]

Unconsciously that mugger causes others to experience his rage. Like creates like. The wave of rage perpetuates, at least until understanding, compassion or even forgiveness take over. Only an enlightened society can stop the wave.

What can we do about this? We, as a society, need to find a way to support parents and families, otherwise we have to accept that the society that we are creating, through the policies and the parties that we vote for in elections, is going to be continually flooded with crime and violence. Locking people up is not the answer.

We would do well to tackle problems as they first arise, in the infant's brain, at a time when it is undergoing the most growth and is therefore most influenced by society. This will take a lot of money. But we have injected unimaginable amounts of cash into the banking system for the benefit of our countries and the world. I'm suggesting that we take the wellbeing of infants as seriously and that we pump considerable resources into ensuring the education of parents and the excellent care and wellbeing of our young. It is crucial to the future of our society and, if we really must place a cost on things, it will be crucial to our economy.

The nations who spend adequately in developing their young will lead the next generation.

WHEN WE KNOW A
MOTHER IS IN DIFFICULTY

When we know of a family member, friend or acquaintance who is having a difficult time with her baby, babies or children, the kind thing to do, then, is help.

It can be especially hard for depressed mothers. Studies show that there's an increased risk of the child of a depressed mother growing up to have emotional problems later in life.[17]

There is always a danger in quoting research of this type and it makes me a little uncomfortable writing it. I feel similarly uncomfortable writing about the negative physiological consequences of long-term depression. Already depressed mothers can feel worse if they think that they may be adversely affecting their babies.

But here is where we, as individuals and as a society, can try to help where we can. It's sometimes better to know how things work than not because then we can do something about it. Where you see a mother struggling, perhaps someone you know, is there something you could do to help her? Maybe she just needs someone to talk to. Or someone to take the infant off her hands for a few hours every now and then to give her a rest.

Your kindness then not only helps the parent but also helps the child. Relieving some of the mother's stress allows her to be more responsive to the needs of her child because she is better rested. And as we offer this kindness, we also help ourselves, improving our own health. We should be grateful, then, for the opportunity to help. And the mother will be grateful to receive it.

The next chapter focuses on gratitude, showing how counting our blessings, whatever they may be, also affects our health.

STORIES OF KINDNESS

Restoring Faith

After my son Calum died, we had help and gifts from so many people, from boxes of homemade cakes left on the doorstep to letters and kind wishes from people we didn't know and hugs from neighbours we had only ever said 'hello' to. We had friends who arrived and made tea, did shopping and offered support. The kindness spread around the world as people heard of our fundraising efforts in aid of research into meningitis, the disease that Calum died of. The band the Fratellis (Calum's favourites) gave us not only a treasured guitar, a painting and a drum skin but also gave us their time, arranged to get my car out of the pound after it got towed away when I went to see them, asked to meet my son's friends, promoted the work of the Meningitis Trust and dedicated their album to Calum. So many other people helped raise funds and wish us well.

A man in the USA entered a competition to win Fratellis goodies for the sole purpose of sending us the items to add to our fundraising efforts. He sent us e-mails with such love and compassion. He was not alone – others did the same. A woman in England sent us some of her treasured collection of Fratellis goodies. More people sold raffle tickets and told their friends about Calum and we received even more good wishes.

I had never before been on the receiving end of such an outpouring of love and kindness. What is so amazing is the effect that this had on me and my family. I have never known darker days – the world was a very bleak place to me at that time. I had lost my love of life as well as my son. These acts of kindness found a way to reach through the veil of tremendous grief and sadness. They created a chink of light that helped me to get through each day and begin to feel that the world was not a bad place. We so often hear of terrible tragedies, misery, fear and anger through our media. We don't often hear of the selfless acts that people do for others.

The people who took the time to write or bake or shop or clean for us are our heroes. The friends who asked how we were and genuinely wanted to know, the ones who listened on the other end of the phone to my sobs at all hours can never be thanked enough. I know they did not do any of these things to be thanked. But it is important for people to know the impact that their kind acts had. These acts were fuel that helped to relight the fire within my soul. They touched a place deep within me that restored my faith in the world. This is not to be taken lightly, as Calum's death made me question everything I had previously believed in.

I doubt if the woman who baked some cakes and left them on our doorstep would have realized the impact that this had. Kindness is so powerful. I have experienced it first-hand. If everyone undertook the task of doing one act of kindness a week, think of how much light that could bring into the world.
Kim

CHAPTER 11

COUNTING BLESSINGS

> **'If you want a strategy to increase your happiness, there's a lot out there that will help. You can take pharmaceuticals, but gratitude is something that doesn't have side effects.'**
> Robert Emmons

Being grateful is an act of kindness to those around us and to the world. It is saying, 'Thank you for being you.' And as it comes from our hearts, it takes the form of recognizing everything that others have contributed to our life. We may show this kindness in words, or just in our minds as we smile and silently recognize people, or in our actions, when we are inspired to act upon the good feelings that well up inside us.

Gratitude is also good for our mental health. It can make us happier. This was the conclusion of a 10-week study involving 196 people that was conducted by psychologists at the University of California at Davis and the University of Miami in 2003.[1]

Once a week, the participants had to write down either five things that had happened in the last week that they were grateful or thankful for (the 'gratitude condition'), five daily hassles (the 'hassles condition') or just five general things that had happened in the past week (the control group, for comparison).

Some of the examples given in the gratitude group included being grateful 'to God for giving me determination', 'for wonderful parents', 'the generosity of friends' and even, 'for waking up this morning'.

Some of the examples in the hassles group included 'Finances depleting quickly', 'Stupid people driving', 'Messy kitchen that no one will clean' and 'Doing a favour for a friend who didn't appreciate it.'

At the end of the 10 weeks, those in the gratitude group were a full 25 per cent happier than those in the hassles group. What we give our attention to really matters. It can make a huge difference to how we feel.

The study also measured optimism, general health as indicated by the participants' number of physical symptoms, and how much exercise they took. Those in the gratitude group were also much more optimistic than those in the hassles group, they had far fewer physical symptoms of illness and they even exercised much more (almost one and a half hours per week more than the hassles group). It seems that a healthier mind encourages us to do healthier things. So not only does counting our blessings make us mentally and emotionally healthier, but it makes us physically healthier too.

Other studies have found the same thing. In one conducted by the same authors, 157 participants were asked to do the exercise every day for two weeks instead of once a week.[2] The 'gratitude group' contained 52 participants, the 'hassles group' contained 49 participants, and there were 56 participants in the control group.

The results were similar. The happiness and wellbeing of those in the gratitude group were much higher than in the hassles group. The study also included a few extra measures of overall well-being. One was how much positive emotion the participants felt. Those in the gratitude group enjoyed significantly more positive emotion in their daily lives than those in the hassles group. In general, participants in the gratitude group were more joyful, excited, energetic, enthusiastic, determined, strong, interested and attentive than those in the hassles group.

In this study there were no measured differences in physical health or time spent exercising, but the scientists wrote that this may have been a consequence of the very short timescale of the study – two weeks versus ten weeks. A longer study would have most likely observed changes in physical health.

An additional blessing from counting blessings is that it also makes us more thoughtful and generous towards others. It makes us better people to be around. This was confirmed by another part of the experiment. Here the researchers asked the participants to report if they had helped people or offered anyone emotional support during the course of the study. It turned out that those in the gratitude group did, in fact, offer help and emotional support to others, which was such a noticeable change in their behaviour that their friends remarked on it. So kindness can be shown in an expression of gratitude, but gratitude also makes us more kind!

Gratitude also helps improve the condition of people suffering from some illnesses. In a gratitude study involving 65 participants with neuromuscular diseases, a gratitude group was compared with a control group.[3] Each person made their list daily for three weeks. Some of the things that the participants listed reflected the support they received from others, including being grateful 'to my paperboy for being so reliable', 'to my boss for under-standing my needs' and 'to my gardener'.

As before, individuals in the gratitude group felt much more posi-tive and satisfied with their lives than those in the control group. They also felt more optimistic and connected with other group participants. They even slept better, felt more refreshed when they woke and suffered less physical pain.

Significantly, many of these benefits were long-lasting. The research team followed up on the participants six months later to see how they were getting on and found that overall wellbeing was still a full 25 per cent higher in the gratitude group than in the control group.

Martin Seligman, a pioneer in the rapidly growing field of posi-tive psychology, found a powerful way of feeling gratitude and showed that expressing it can have a monumental impact upon people. In a study conducted by Seligman and his colleagues at the University of Pennsylvania, participants were asked to write and personally deliver a letter of gratitude to someone who had been really kind to them or had made a really positive difference in their lives. It might have been, for instance, a parent, another family member, a friend or a medical practitioner who had saved their life. But when they delivered the letter, they had to read it aloud to the person.

This was life-changing for some of the participants. One week after the letter was delivered, participants in the gratitude group were happier and less depressed than before. And these benefits were still being enjoyed after one month when the participants checked in and once again reported on how they were feeling.[4]

Counting our blessings has a huge impact upon our lives. So few of us realize this and so many of us become immersed in complaining about life, our job, the state of our home, our partner, even our internet connection. While some of these complaints are valid, the positive state and increased personal energy that gratitude brings helps us to approach situations like these in a more positive, optimistic, confident and direct way. And sometimes things even have a funny way of resolving themselves when we're feeling positive.

FREQUENCY MATTERS

Studies show that the type of gratitude exercise we do and how often we do it matters. In a study reported in 2005 in the journal *Review of General Psychology*, participants were asked to think about things they were grateful for either once a week or three times a week for six weeks.[5]

As with other studies, those in the gratitude group got healthier. Overall wellbeing improved compared with the control group. However, one thing was different: this time only those who did the exercise once a week enjoyed the benefits. Those who did it three times a week didn't. It turned out that it wasn't that they were doing the exercise too much, it was that the type of gratitude exercise they were doing didn't lend itself to being done too often.

In some gratitude studies, participants are encouraged to think only of the things that they are grateful for that have happened in the past 24 hours or the past week. But this study asked participants to generally list things that they were grateful for. For instance, one might write, 'My mum, dad, sisters, etc.' But then they might find themselves writing the same things again a few days later.

When we list everything in our lives that we're grateful for too often it can become boring after a while. Rewriting, 'I am grateful for the help my mum gave me,' for instance, three times a week can reduce how much we really feel the gratitude. It's OK the first few times, but after that the impact is less. Indeed, a 1991 study showed that thinking about an event over and over again reduces its impact, making it feel more familiar and even explainable, which is great if it's a negative event. But it causes us to take positive things for granted.[6]

This is why regular gratitude exercises should have us listing things that have happened in the past 24 hours or the past week. If we're writing the same stuff each time then we need to leave some time between doing it – at least a month, I'd say.

COMPLAINING FEELS GOOD, BUT ONLY FOR A FEW MINUTES

Gratitude studies that include a group that focuses on hassles allow us to see just how destructive complaining can be for our mental and physical health. In the first gratitude study reported in this chapter, the difference in happiness between the gratitude group and the hassles group was 25 per cent.

Complaining has become a habit for many people. Any technique that can help us to break that habit would be a health-giver for many. That's why I love the concept of 'a complaint-free world', promoted by Will Bowen in his excellent book of the same name that I mentioned earlier. Not only is it great for relationships with people, but for your relationship with life. It can make you feel much happier.

Bowen encourages people to wear a purple 'complaint-free' wristband and take up the challenge of going 21 days without complaining, moaning, criticizing or even unfairly judging someone or something. Each time we complain, moan, criticize or unfairly judge, we have to move the band to the other wrist. It really makes us aware of how we behave, especially when we have to move it a half dozen times an hour. And it's an eye-opener for many.

When they first get their band, most people have to change it to the other wrist several times in the first hour and throughout the day. But quite soon many are able to easily go three or four days without a single complaint. Then magic happens. People suddenly realize how much better they feel when they're not complaining and how much happier those around them seem to be too.

Can we really make others miserable? Yes. Complaining sets others off too. When you stop, they often revert to a positive state.

Although it is only a 21-day challenge, this becomes a lifelong change for many. With practice, you quickly learn to catch yourself on the cusp of a complaint or a criticism and become skilled at rephrasing what you say, learning that choosing to say something constructive instead of complaining is better for everyone, and you get better results in life.

Sitting at lunch one day, a woman was about to complain to the waiter that her soup was cold. I had been speaking at a conference that morning and had just finished giving a talk during which, at one stage, I had mentioned the complaint-free concept. Gesturing towards her soup, she insisted to me that, regardless of what I had said in my talk, sometimes you just had to complain. She was about to display her annoyance about the soup to the waiter but, on seeing my facial expression, she asked me what I would do.

I pointed out that there were many different ways to communicate the same thing and that I was sure that she could get her point across without complaining. I suggested that she could try something along the lines of, 'Excuse me. I wonder if you could help? Would you be able to bring me a warm plate of soup, or even have this plate heated up? It's a wee bit cold.' This way, it would be possible to communicate that the soup was cold without complaining to the waiter. My experience is that when you communicate like this, people (and waiters) tend to do more for you. And you feel better for it in the long term.

OK, offloading is therapeutic at times. But for many people, it's become too much of a habit. And it's a habit that needs to be broken, for the sake of better mental, emotional and physical health, not only for those complaining but for those around them too.

YOU'LL BE COUNTING YOUR BLESSINGS 'TIL YOU'RE 100

Gratitude even makes us live longer.

It's true. We know, for instance, that optimists live longer than pessimists. A 30-year study conducted by scientists at the Mayo Clinic in the USA, involving 447 people, found that optimists had about 50 per cent less risk of early death than pessimists.[7]

And having a positive attitude impacts longevity too. A 660-person study conducted by scientists at Yale University and published in 2002 found that those who had the most positive attitudes about ageing lived, on average, around 7.5 years longer than those with the most negative attitudes.[8]

In another study, psychologists at UCLA studied the attitudes of 78 men with AIDS in the 1980s. Those who were more optimistic lived around nine months longer than those who had a more 'realistic' view of their condition and prognosis.[9]

When I worked in the pharmaceutical industry I learned that the company I worked for packaged anti-cancer drugs differently for the Japanese market. In Japan, the families of terminally ill patients are allowed to elect not to tell them that they are terminal. The knowledge that a person is terminal often speeds up their decline. Not knowing helps many to live longer.

A negative attitude generally creates stress in the mind and body. Over a long period of time, it produces oxidative stress and inflammation and shortens our telomeres. Anger and stress can dampen the immune system and hostility increases the risk of heart disease. Gratitude, on the other hand, is an antidote to all of these things. By protecting us from stress, anger and hostility, and therefore the negative consequences of them, it helps us live longer.

The 'nun study' is a well-known longevity study where the Sisters of Notre Dame wrote about their lives when first entering a convent as young women. When their autobiographies were reviewed by psychologists 60 years later, it turned out that those whose writing contained more positivity, showing thankfulness and, for many, an attitude of seeing their life as a gift, and whose writing reflected the most hope, love and contentment, lived a whole six to ten years longer than those whose writing reflected more negativity.[10]

COUNT BLESSINGS INSTEAD OF SHEEP

Counting blessings is a really good way of getting to sleep. It's especially good for those times when you wake in the middle of the night and your mind is racing, or for people who just can't sleep.

In a 2009 study conducted by psychologists at the University of Manchester, 401 people filled out questionnaires about sleep quality and gratitude in their life. Those who scored highest on gratitude also had better sleep quality, longer sleep duration, got to sleep more quickly and had less daytime dysfunction.[11]

In one of the studies conducted by Robert Emmons, a psychologist and leader in the field of gratitude research, it was found that participants who did gratitude exercises got to sleep better at night. So convinced was Emmons about the power of gratitude for this that he wrote, in his excellent book *Thanks*, 'If you want to sleep more soundly, count blessings, not sheep.'[12]

At a weekend retreat that I ran, I discussed this on the Saturday afternoon. The retreat had begun on the Friday night and a woman in the group had told me on the Saturday morning that she hadn't slept the previous night but that this was normal for her. So I shared some of the gratitude research and asked the whole group to do a gratitude exercise before going to sleep, preferably as they lay in bed. I asked them to just think of five to ten things that they were grateful for that had happened that day.

Next morning, most reported that they had really enjoyed the exercise and were going to keep it up. Some felt it was an excellent way of going to sleep feeling peaceful and positive rather than thinking of worries. Some felt it would be a good way to finish the day on a positive note, especially if they'd watched TV late at night. The woman who usually couldn't sleep was positively beaming. She'd slept soundly all night and said that it was the first time she'd slept that well for years. And she hadn't even been in the comfort of her own bed, but staying in a holistic centre miles from home.

GRATEFUL CHILDREN

Gratitude exercises are good for children too, at least when they're old enough to understand what gratitude is. A 2008 study conducted by psychologists at Hofstra University, New York, and the University of California at Davis compared gratitude with hassles for 221 students in the sixth and seventh grades. They found that those in the gratitude group experienced much less negative emotion and were more optimistic about the following week than those in the hassles group.[13]

The students were also healthier. They reported less sickness and were 'less bothered with physical problems'. The gratitude group also reported feeling more gratitude for kindness shown to them by others.

In addition, the gratitude group was much more satisfied with school and life. This is one of the things that gratitude brings out in us – it helps us become more accepting of and satisfied with what we have. The grass becomes greener on our own side of the fence.

YOU'LL FEEL HAPPIER WHEN YOU NOTICE THE GREEN IN YOUR OWN GRASS

The grass is always greener on the other side for many people. We compare what we have to what others have, or to what we see on TV or in magazines, and all of a sudden the things we have aren't good enough any more. We want the same as everyone else, or even better.

Psychologists call these 'upward comparisons'. We look upwards to what we think is better than what we have, whether that be possessions or personal qualities. But studies show that upward comparisons are not so good for our health. They make us more negative and unhappy. They even create resentment and can make us feel depressed.

In some gratitude studies, upward comparison groups are actually used to show how powerful gratitude is. In these studies, participants write down, say, five things that they don't have but that they wish they had. But when they make these comparisons, they feel much less happiness, joy and gratefulness than participants in the studies who count their blessings.[14]

So often we convince ourselves that we really do need the stuff that we see, that it will make us more relaxed, satisfied and happier. And it's true for a while – when we get the stuff, we really do feel happier. But how long does it last? We eventually get used to it, or adapt to it, as psychologists say, and so something else catches our attention that we believe will return the peace or happiness to us. It's a sure-fire way of getting rid of any extra money you might have.

Of course there are times when we really do need the stuff. But more often than not, we want new things just because the new model is shinier, or faster, or bigger, or smaller, or prettier, or has a few extra gadgets. There's real power, instead, in reflecting on the good that comes from what we have now, in finding some appreciation of our current circumstances. It's ultimately better for our finances and is the ideal tonic in challenging economic times.

Counting our blessings helps us appreciate the things that we already have rather than seeing them and the people in our lives as disposable. We start to see things we've never noticed before and gradually feelings of unhappiness or dissatisfaction are replaced with happiness and satisfaction.

One study tested the effects of making comparisons on satisfaction.[15] Satisfaction is a measure that shows that we are pretty comfortable or at peace with our life situation, which may be where we live, the house we live in, our job, our relationships or even ourselves. The studies clearly showed that satisfaction has much less to do with actual situations than most people think. It turns out it has more to do with how we *think* about our life situations.

In the study, participants were asked to complete the sentences 'I wish I was _____' or 'I'm glad I'm not _____.' Satisfaction was measured before they did this and again at the end.

Those who were glad they were *not* something were much more satisfied than before, meaning that they were happier with their life than they had been a few moments before. They had gone up the scale of satisfaction.

But when participants listed things that they wished they were, in a way making themselves feel inadequate and comparing their lives now to what they could be, they turned out to feel less satisfied with life. They slid down the scale.

Of course, making comparisons like this is useful when generating the motivation that we need to pursue our goals. Being less satisfied with an area of our lives motivates us to change it. But I think we make upward comparisons just too often, which leads to chronic dissatisfaction and unhappiness in our lives.

It's not so much our lives, but the thoughts we think *about* our lives that count. Try seeing what you have through different eyes. You might be surprised with what you find.

In the words of the writer Melody Beattie:

'Gratitude unlocks the fullness of life. It turns what we have into enough, and more. It turns denial into acceptance, chaos into order, confusion into clarity... It turns problems into gifts, failures into success, the unexpected into perfect timing, and mistakes into important events. Gratitude makes sense of our past, brings peace for today and creates a vision for tomorrow.'[16]

REMEMBERING POSITIVE THINGS

Many people have felt that their life was on a downward spiral at one time or another. Many are in that place right now. But studies suggest that gratitude can actually put us on an upward spiral. It helps us remember the positive things in our lives more than the negative ones, so is known as a 'positive recall bias'.[17]

Many of us are all too aware that when we feel low and our hearts are heavy with negative emotions, all we seem to remember is the negative stuff – the wrong choices, the mistakes we've made. But our memories often just confirm what we are thinking right now. When we feel different, we remember different things. When we're positive, we remember more positive things. It's an upward or downward spiral that's almost always down to how we feel right now.

In the brain, by putting us in a positive state, gratitude strengthens neural connections to positive memories and experiences and even enhances the forming of positive memories. In time, these neural pathways become dominant and feeling positive gradually becomes a more permanent state.

In a sense, gratitude impacts us at the genetic level by activating genes that provide the proteins that forge neural connections around positive memories.

IMPROVING RELATIONSHIPS

Gratitude also builds relationships. It brings us closer to people who have done good things for us. This was shown in a 2008 study that took place in a University of Virginia sorority.[18] During a gift-giving week known as 'Big Sister Week', older members of the sorority give gifts to new members as a way of welcoming them and bringing them into the fold of the larger group. During the Big Sister Week in the study, 78 'big sisters' had gifts delivered to 82 'little sisters', they organized events for them and they ensured that the little sisters were pampered throughout the week. This was done anonymously until the end of the week, when the big sisters revealed their identity.

At the end of the week and again one month later, psychologists from the University of Virginia asked the little sisters to report on the benefits they received during the week and asked both big sisters and little sisters to report on their relationships after the week ended.

The results showed that gratitude built relationships. Those little sisters who felt most gratitude for the gifts given to them enjoyed a better quality of relationship with the big sisters who had given them the gifts and felt more integrated into the sorority.

Gratitude is especially important in our relationships with our loved ones, where time causes us to forget much of the good they have brought into our lives. Many people in long-term relationships learn to take their partner for granted. Living with them every day and getting caught up in the challenges and circumstances of life causes them to forget how important the other person is to them and they sometimes remember only when it is too late.

Practising gratitude helps us see the beauty in our intimate relationships and also in our friendships. We start to recall things we'd forgotten but that were significant at the time. Then kind acts blossom once more. We start to show more care and attentiveness towards our partners and friends. Kindness begets gratitude and gratitude begets kindness. It is a beautiful circle.

Some psychologists can predict whether a marriage will last the next few years by studying the ratio of positivity to negativity in how each partner thinks about or relates to the other. The 'magic ratio', according to psychologist John Gottman, is five positives for every negative. In a study of 700 newly-wed couples, Gottman and his colleagues observed each couple speaking together for 15 minutes and scored their positive to negative ratio. Then they predicted who would still be together or divorced 10 years later. They were 94 per cent correct.[19]

When we practise gratitude, our level of positivity rises to a level that ensures the survival of a relationship and allows many couples to experience a new honeymoon period.

LIFE IS A GIFT

'As each day comes to us refreshed and anew, so does my gratitude renew itself daily. The breaking of the sun over the horizon is my grateful heart dawning upon a blessed world.'

Adabella Radici

Some people see their life as a gift. They see the people in their life as gifts and the moment-by-moment experiences as gifts, and they accept all of them with gratitude. There is now mounting scientific evidence that seeing life in this way is good for us. It affects the balance of stress hormones and pro-inflammatory cytokines in our bloodstream, it affects our heart and immune system, and it even affects the chemistry and structure of our brain.

You don't have to be religious to consider life as a gift. Many religious people or spiritual people do see life as a gift, and it probably contributes to why they tend to be, on the whole, healthier than non-religious or non-spiritual people. But a person can have no spiritual views and still choose to think of each day as a gift. And it brings the same benefits as standard gratitude exercises.

In one study, Robert Emmons found that viewing events in life as gifts produced as much gain in wellbeing as a standard gratitude exercise.[20]

BETTER THAN PROZAC

Some studies have linked gratitude, or the lack of it, with depression. Some have found that the more depressed a person is, the less grateful they generally feel, and vice versa. More gratitude equates to less depression. Gratitude and depression are at opposite ends of a seesaw. As gratitude goes up, depression typically comes down. And as depression goes up, gratitude comes down.

In a 2004 study, psychologists at Eastern Washington University found that people who were clinically depressed showed almost 50 per cent less gratitude than a control group which was not depressed.[21]

Some even stronger evidence for the link between depression and the absence of gratitude comes from studies of identical twins separated at birth. Such twins are often used in studies because they have the same genes but grow up in different environments. So scientists can delete out the influence of genetics and get a picture of the other factors that are influencing health. So, for example, if one twin is brought up to count their blessings more than the other then differences in rates of depression can be linked with gratitude and not be genetic.

Twin studies have found that being grateful is indeed linked with a lower risk of depression. Twins who are the most grateful tend to have the fewest depressive symptoms and those with the most depressive symptoms tend to be least grateful.[22]

The reason why gratitude can be an antidote to depression lies in the fact that depressed people focus more of their attention on themselves (not in a selfish, egotistical way but on their personal pain) than on others, which is understandable. But gratitude automatically takes attention away from the self and focuses it on others. This is why it can alleviate depression.

While this isn't an absolute truth, because depression can come in many forms and have many causes, counting blessings does seem to be able to protect us from it. Some people find that doing a daily gratitude intervention makes them feel better in the long term than taking antidepressants.

GOOD FOR THE HEART

Just like good relationships, gratitude is cardioprotective, especially for people who have had a heart attack.

This is what a 1987 University of Connecticut study found.[23] Studying patients who had had a heart attack, psychologists found that those who saw benefits from the attack, including appreciating life more or seeing it as a gift, were much less likely to have another heart attack over the next eight years than those who blamed their heart attack on others. Those who blamed had a much higher risk of having another heart attack. Seeing benefits in their experience was protective. Blaming was destructive.

As we know from earlier in the book, having close bonds with people is good for the heart. But having close bonds *and* a grateful disposition can be a health-giving elixir.

In one study, scientists asked 3,000 patients with significant coronary blockage if they counted their blessings and had social support. The results implied that counting blessings and social support offered some degree of protection against heart disease. It was clear that those who had greatest blockage and had little social contact were the ones who happened to be less likely to count their blessings. Those who had social contact and counted their blessings had least blockage.[24]

IT'LL HURT LESS IF YOU'RE THANKFUL

Gratitude even helps us when we are in pain. This was shown by a 28-day study conducted at San Luis Hospital in California. Chronic pain sufferers were asked to perform a daily gratitude meditation in which they were asked to feel a sense of deep gratitude for things in their lives that they deeply appreciated. At the end of the four weeks, there was a significant drop in the pain experienced by the sufferers.[25]

Gratitude can reduce pain in two ways. The first is that it helps distract us from the pain. As more of our focus becomes dominated by what we're thankful for, less attention is present on the pain. But second is that studies have shown that positive emotions can be analgesics. It is believed that gratitude causes the release of the brain's own version of morphine (endorphin) in the brain and this physically blocks pain signals.

Norman Cousins, while a professor of Medical Humanities at the University of California, Los Angeles, suffered from a debilitating illness (ankylosing spondylitis, which is a form of arthritis) that left him in almost constant and severe pain. He discovered that a positive attitude, love, faith and hope, coupled with watching Marx Brothers films that made him laugh hard, were his recipe for a full recovery.

In his bestselling book, *Anatomy of an Illness*, he wrote, 'I made the joyous discovery that ten minutes of genuine belly laughter had an anaesthetic effect and gave me at least two hours pain-free sleep.'[26]

Laughter, like positive emotions, produces pain-blocking endorphins in the brain.

Similarly, in a 1998 study published in the journal *Pain*, volunteers watched either humorous, Holocaust or neutral films and then took a pain tolerance test. Those who had watched the humorous films had a greater pain tolerance than those who had watched the other films.[27]

A personal observation of mine is that, as well as making us feel positive, gratitude actually allows us to experience more humour. I have noticed that it is an antidote to some of the mental and emotional worries that fill our minds. These almost constant preoccupations cause us to take our days much too seriously and to forget to look around us at the life that is happening. Many people can go days at a time with their minds filled with hassles, worries and concerns, and rarely notice that they have missed numerous opportunities to smile or laugh.

When gratitude becomes a habit, we do stop and notice life more. This allows us to have more enriching experiences with those around us because we are much less distracted by worries. And when this happens, we laugh more. An act of kindness towards someone, then, might be to help them to laugh!

FINDING A PATH THROUGH
THE DIFFICULT TIMES

Studies have shown that gratitude is a powerful coping strategy for life's difficult times. It has been demonstrated that it helps us navigate a way through panic attacks, coping with poverty, caring for Alzheimer's sufferers, looking after children with disabilities, the trials and tribulations of parenthood and even natural disasters. It increases our positive emotions, which push some of the negative emotions out of our heads. It is not possible to be positive and negative at the same time. In the brain, it's one or the other. And in helping us feel more positive, gratitude dampens some of the stresses of difficult times and helps us find a way through.

In a study of relatives of people with Alzheimer's, for instance, half wrote what they felt grateful for each day in a gratitude journal and half made a list of their daily hardships. At the end of the study, those who had written in gratitude journals reported greater overall wellbeing and also less stress and depression.[28]

One of the beauties of gratitude is that we begin to take pleasure in small things that we ordinarily forget to notice. In the study, it was found that some of those in the gratitude group began to celebrate small victories, like being called by name by the Alzheimer's sufferer, for instance. In the stresses and worries that saturate our minds when we are under pressure and feel overwhelmed, these small things almost always go unnoticed. But they are actually the seeds of inner happiness.

As we learned in an earlier chapter, the carers of Alzheimer's patients who suffer the most stress have the shortest telomeres and age the fastest. Gratitude, then, is an antidote to stress and ageing. It can slow the ageing process.

ALL BY MYSELF

'When eating bamboo sprouts, remember the man who planted them.'

Chinese proverb

When we achieve goals, there have almost always been a number of people involved, each, often unknowingly, contributing a small brick in the wall of our success. It does us good to acknowledge people and to be grateful for their role in our life. And of course it is a display of kindness.

For instance, I consider having my first book published by Hay House UK in 2006 one of my successes. I spent two years researching and collating information and tirelessly condensing scientific jargon into an easy-to-understand book. Then I went through several rejections from publishers and finally self-published before, seven months later, Hay House offered to publish it. It would be easy to pat myself on the back for seeing it through from start to finish, for having kept myself going when times were really hard, especially when the rejection letters were mounting up. Yes, I worked hard and kept focused on my goal, but many others played a role that I would never like to forget.

My partner, Elizabeth, for instance, was instrumental in so many ways. For most of the first year of writing, I had little income. Rather than urge me to earn, Elizabeth took several jobs that she hated. At times, she had to walk around town centres for about five hours a day handing out leaflets, often in the rain, suffering the embarrassment (she would only do it in places far from home in case anyone recognized her), while I sat in the warmth of coffee shops nearby, drinking coffee and eating pastries as I wrote. She never once put any pressure on me to get a 'real' job. And she so longed for success in her own career as an actress and scriptwriter, even an *opportunity* to fulfil her dreams, which would have been easier if we had had less financial pressure, which I could have relieved if I had had an income.

And when I received one rejection letter after another, it was Elizabeth who encouraged me to keep going because she knew how much my dream meant to me. It was her idea that I self-publish.

There was a time when I almost gave up. I nearly went back to the pharmaceutical industry, being tempted by a potentially lucrative position that would have eased all of our financial pressures and almost certainly created the space that Elizabeth needed to pursue her dreams. Yet she talked me out of it and encouraged me to keep striving.

And so it was that Elizabeth's unwavering support was instrumental in me writing this very book, as well as the three others that came before it. For this, and much more, I look with deep gratitude to her. It would never have worked without her.

I also deeply acknowledge the role that my mum, dad and sisters played, as well as Elizabeth's parents. Their love and support have helped me in so many ways that it would require another book just to write it all down.

The point is that when we really think about it, we start to see the parts others play in our life. We see that the tapestry of our life has many threads, and these threads have been woven by many people. Remove one thread and a hole appears in the fabric. Without the input of certain people, our life would rarely turn out to be what it is.

It is healthy for us, and for our relationships with others, to acknowledge the blessings people bring to our life. And, of course, it is a gift to them that we notice and appreciate them.

It can be a powerful exercise to consider how things might have turned out for us if certain people hadn't been in our life. A 2008 study actually asked participants to consider: 'What if it had never happened?'[29] It asked them to write about why a positive event might never have happened and why it was surprising that it did. Another part of the experiment turned the focus towards romantic partners, considering the consequences of having never met them.

The results clearly showed that focusing on imagining if something had never happened, whether it was a life event or the presence of a romantic partner, made people much more satisfied with their lives. For many, this was a more powerful exercise than actually contemplating positives in their lives. By realizing that it could have turned out differently, they valued what they had even more.

For the sake of your own health, happiness and relationships, and the health and happiness of your loved ones, make a point of counting your blessings more. If you need some guidelines, here are a few suggestions:

TIPS FOR CREATING AN ATTITUDE OF GRATITUDE
- Keep a gratitude journal. Write in it regularly. Each time you feel grateful for something, add it to your journal. For periods of time, make it a daily practice to list five to ten things that happened in the last 24 hours that you are grateful for. Or fill out your journal once a week with all that you have been grateful for in the past week.

- Think of the people in your life and spend time considering how each of them has contributed to your life. Spend a short time on a different person each day until you have gone through all of the people who are important to you. When you finish, you may even want to try the exercise for people with whom you don't get on.

- Write a letter of gratitude to someone who has influenced your life. Hand-deliver it and read it aloud to them.

- Pay attention to the small things. It will help you to develop a much greater sense of appreciation and present-moment awareness.

- Re-evaluate some of your successes and consider the role that others played in them. You may even wish to thank them for it: 'You know, I never did thank you for...'

Gratitude research is showing that gratitude brings us a more loving feeling, as well as more joy, enthusiasm, happiness, optimism and even better physical health. We feel more connected and our relationships improve. Robert Emmons points out that gratitude also reduces destructive impulses like greed, envy, resentment, bitterness and hostility and helps us to cope better with the stresses and strains of everyday life. Show me a drug that can do all this in a one-tablet-a-day form!

Gratitude, as a daily practice, can produce this reward. Then, through this daily practice, and the happiness we gain from it, our goals and dreams flow towards us with much less effort. Our relationships improve, our network of positive social interactions expands, oxytocin increases, protecting us from heart disease, our friendships deepen, our job and finances improve, and life generally takes a turn for the better.

Seeing life experiences as gifts is a nice way to boost happiness. Some religions encourage the cultivation of this attitude. When we have it, we feel somehow rewarded, blessed. Our self-esteem rises and we feel happier. Training ourselves to view life like this is a sure-fire way of becoming happier.

Some religions and spiritual traditions believe that consciously feeling gratitude is a mark of spiritual maturity. If spiritual evolution is the next stage for humanity, and perhaps it is, considering that the prefrontal cortex is the most recently evolved part of the human brain and is active in states of compassion, gratitude and spiritual contemplation, then we should all be aspiring to become more compassionate, kind and grateful. Practices that help us to do so will take us on to the next level of social development, where we will cooperate more, share more, trust more, forgive more and witness more peace and happiness and kindness in the world.

STORIES OF KINDNESS

A Spotless Room

I woke up in my hotel room and threw the covers off the bed. I didn't bother making the bed, as I knew the chambermaid would do it. I went into the bathroom and noticed a wooden holder with a range of shampoo, conditioner, shower gel and hand cream in it. I thought how nice it was and decided that I would slip it in my bag and take it all home with me.

As I was packing my bag, I thought to myself, 'Why do I want to take more toiletries? I've got loads at home!' I then wondered how many times the chambermaid had to replace things that were taken from the room and thought about how hard she must have to work cleaning up after people. So I decided that I would do all the cleaning for her!

I popped out and bought some cleaning fluid and cloths. I cleaned the bathroom, stripped and folded the bedding, cleaned the kettle, cups, spoons and tray, cleaned the mirrors and windowsills, picked up every bit of mess I could see on the carpet, emptied the bin into a plastic bag and tied it up. It took me an hour, but looked really good. I then left a thank-you card and £5 tip, and I wrote the words: 'Thank you for all the hard work you do.'

On my way home I felt great. I wondered what the chambermaid had thought when she'd seen how clean the room was and I kept grinning to myself. It felt fantastic! **Linzi**

CHAPTER 12

LETTING GO OF THE PAST

> 'Forgiveness is the moment-to-moment experience of peace and understanding that occurs when an injured party's suffering is reduced as they transform their grievance against an offending party.'
>
> Fred Luskin, PhD, from
> *Forgive for Good*

Forgiveness isn't always the answer!

This might seem like a strange way to start a chapter on forgiveness in a book called *Why Kindness is Good for You*, but wounds can sometimes be so deep and hurt so unbearably that forgiveness just isn't possible. Sometimes, seeking justice or retribution is all that keeps people going. Feeling that justice has been done can be the only thing that brings them closure. That way they feel that they have gained some compensation for what they have lost or have obtained a mark of respect for the person they have lost.

We should not try to force people to forgive. Forgiveness is a personal choice and a journey that people have to make by themselves, if ever.

Gabriel Ferez and his friend, Laurent Bonomo, were tortured to death in their London apartment by a serial offender and a heroin addict. On jailing the offenders for 35 and 40 years, the judge, Mr Justice Saunders, said, 'These are the worst crimes I have ever had to deal with.' The words of Olivier Ferez, Gabriel's father, were printed on the front page of the *Metro* newspaper in the UK on Friday 5 June 2009. He said:

'I might tell you that every morning, on my way to work, I cry, always at the same hour. I no longer know how to answer people when they ask how many children I have.

'I might tell you that I do not sleep at night and I fill it with the sound of the radio to occupy my mind and stop thinking. I might tell you that I feel ashamed of laughing now.

'I might tell you that I look elsewhere whenever I come across the sight of a wedding, of other people's happiness, because the display of their joy is like so many stab wounds to my heart.

'This is now what my daily life is like. No child, no individual, should have to put up with such barbarity.'

The knowledge of your child suffering so severely is beyond comprehension for most people. If Mr Ferez ever chooses to forgive, then that is something private between him and his own thoughts and it is not for anyone to give him their idea of the moral high road.

Sometimes, revenge actually feels like the best course of action and produces the only sense of peace that a suffering person can get. Some studies have even suggested that people whose partners have been sexually unfaithful towards them might recover more quickly if they were to dish out some form of emotional revenge on their partner.[1]

One of my friends was once left by her partner, a teacher who had an affair with one of his pupils, whom he subsequently married. She wasn't over it until five years later, when he rang up out of the blue to say his wife had had an affair and left *him*. Then all of a sudden she was fine. She told me it was quite scary to realize how much she had simply been wanting retribution! Now, 15 years later, the couple are both with other people and are in friendly and affectionate e-mail contact with each other. And they both agree that his wife leaving him was an emotional awakening for him and set my friend on the road to recovery. Revenge, even if inadvertently dished out by someone else, can be therapeutic.

WHEN FORGIVENESS IS POSSIBLE, IT CAN HEAL MAJOR PAIN

When a person is in a place in their life where they can entertain the possibility of forgiveness, however, it can be health-giving for them. It is a form of kindness to the self.

Immaculée Ilibagiza is a survivor of the 1994 Rwandan holocaust where over a million of the Tutsi tribe that she belonged to were killed in a state-sponsored massacre. She hid for 91 days inside a tiny bathroom with seven women while murderers who had slain her parents, most of her brothers and all of the Tutsis in the village prowled around chanting her name. She speaks of forgiveness in her intensely moving book *Left to Tell*.

In it, she describes how she was confronted by one of the ring-leaders who had personally killed her father, during a visit to a prison where he was being held. Despite the extreme pain of having had most of her close, loving family murdered, she writes:

'He was sobbing. I could feel his shame. He looked up at me for only a moment, but our eyes met. I reached out, touched his hands lightly, and quietly said what I'd come to say: "I forgive you."

'My heart eased immediately, and I could see the tension release in his shoulders.'[2]

There has been a great deal of research into forgiveness that shows us why it's good for us. In 2000, for example, five women from Northern Ireland (three Protestant and two Catholic), who had suffered the tragic loss of their sons, were invited to participate in the Stanford–Northern Ireland HOPE project led by Dr Fred Luskin of Stanford University.[3]

At the beginning of the study, Luskin's team measured the women's level of hurt at an average of 8.6 on a scale of 1–10. Then they were given training that taught them how to forgive and also how forgiveness would benefit their health. This can be a motivating factor for many people. Indeed, after the training, the women registered only 3.6 on the hurt scale – a massive change. And when they were interviewed six months later, the change had stayed with them.

The study also measured anger, stress and depression, which all accompany hurt. It found that anger levels also reduced because of the training, dropping by 23 per cent from 21.6 to 16.6 on the anger scale. Stress was also significantly reduced and the women became much less depressed. When forgiveness was actually measured using the Rye Forgiveness Scale, where the women had to agree or disagree with a range of questions like 'I can't stop thinking about how I was wronged by this person', it increased from 37 to 53 points and stabilized at 51 after six months. An additional by-product was that the forgiveness training even helped the women to become more optimistic. They had more hope for the future.

Building on the results of the HOPE project, Luskin and his team then created HOPE 2 and this time invited 17 men from Northern Ireland (eight Protestants and nine Catholics), who had also suffered the loss of an immediate family member (parents, siblings, spouses or sons or daughters), to participate. They went through seven days of group forgiveness training.

As with the women before them, forgiveness was the solution to much of their pain. On the hurt scale, levels dropped an average of 1.7 points, from 6.5 to 4.1. Although this was not as much as the women's score, it was still a significant drop. Similarly, anger, stress and depression also reduced. The men even reported an increase in physical vitality (energy level, appetite, sleep patterns and general wellbeing).

On the forgiveness scale, 15 of them showed substantial gains in forgiveness, although 2 of them showed less forgiveness.[4]

This reminds us that although forgiveness is intensely healing, it is not for everyone at all times.

HEALING MORE COMMON HURTS

Most people don't have major hurts in life that involve the violent loss of a loved one or some form of abuse. What fills most hearts is the offences and betrayals that they experience. A 2005 study examined forgiveness in 55 Stanford University students who had an unresolved interpersonal hurt that did not include violence or sexual abuse and who were open to the possibility of forgiveness.[5]

The participants were put into three groups, two of which were given forgiveness training while one served as a control. The forgiveness groups received their forgiveness training for one hour at a time on a weekly basis for six weeks and, just like in the HOPE project, they were then assessed for changes in anger, hurt and forgiveness. They were also assessed ten weeks further on to see if any beneficial changes had stayed with them.

The study showed that those who had received the forgiveness training were on average 15 per cent less angry afterwards in terms of how they reacted to being provoked, which was measured as 'angry reaction'. They also showed a 20 per cent reduction in their general tendency to anger, known as 'state anger'.

Hurt is something that often lingers for a long time after the event in question. Yet after the forgiveness training, this was much less too.

Those who received the training also became much more forgiving towards those who had hurt them. One of the things the study measured was how much malice and estrangement they felt towards those who had hurt them. The women in the study, 75 per cent of the participants, experienced much less malice and estrangement towards their offender after the training. It was especially noted that their levels of malice towards the offender became very low: a significant achievement.

Another measure of the study was that at the beginning the treatment group only showed a very small willingness to forgive, which is normal. Unless we are motivated, forgiveness is rarely the first thing on our minds, because it feels as though we're letting someone off the hook. Yet after the forgiveness training, which not only included education in how to forgive but also about how good forgiving can be for us, they were much more willing to forgive in the future.

A final observation in the study was that the participants showed much more hopefulness at the end and they were much better – skilled even – at managing their emotions and future interpersonal hurts.

A larger Stanford forgiveness study, involving 259 people with an unresolved hurt, gave the training to a large group in six 90-minute sessions.[6] It taught them to take less personal offence, to develop a better understanding of their offender and themselves, and also to blame the offender less. It not only helped them forgive their offender, but the results showed that they were, on average, 70 per cent less hurt than before the training, and this was still the same after six months. They were much less stressed and angry and, as with the other studies, they even reported being more optimistic.

People who go through forgiveness training learn that they can only move forward when they let go of the past. Pain and grudges should stay in the past where they belong. The future is forwards, not backwards.

GOOD FOR THE HEART

We know from earlier chapters that anger and hostility, which can grow out of holding a grudge, can increase blood pressure and lead to heart disease. And stress is a major risk factor in heart disease.

In one study, 20 individuals who were enjoying happy relationships were compared with 20 couples in troubled relationships. Those in the troubled relationships had higher levels of cortisol in their bloodstream, which is a marker of stress. And the levels increased further when those in the troubled relationships even thought about their relationship.[7]

Forgiveness reduces stress and helps us release grudges and is therefore good for the heart. In 1992, scientists at the University of Wisconsin studied 36 men with coronary artery disease and who also had unresolved psychological stress that was related to a domestic conflict, childhood, work or war. The men who received forgiveness training were found to have improved blood flow to the heart.[8]

In a 2001 study conducted by psychologists at Hope College in Holland, 71 people were asked to either think of hurtful memories and grudges or imagine granting forgiveness and take an empathic perspective. Those who had to think of the hurtful memories and grudges immediately registered higher blood pressure and increased heart rates. Those who imagined forgiveness, on the other hand, had comparatively much lower blood pressure and heart rate.[9]

A 2007 study of 99 participants also equated forgiveness with lower blood pressure and the authors even suggested that forgiveness might aid in the recovery of the heart after stress.[10]

A 2003 study found that people who had suffered a heart attack and went through a 10-hour course in forgiveness had improved coronary function.[11]

And in a 2006 study of 25 hypertensive people who experienced high levels of anger, forgiveness training over eight weeks also produced significant reductions in their blood pressure.[12]

There is no doubt that forgiveness not only heals the emotional heart but that it heals the physical heart too. With this knowledge, forgiveness then becomes a display of kindness towards ourselves, something that we often forget about.

WHEN GRUDGES BUILD UP AT WORK

The workplace is where many people build up grudges towards others. Another Stanford study looked at the effects of forgiving in a workplace environment.[13] The researchers examined the effects of forgiveness training on sales performance and on quality of life in 104 people in the financial services industry, which was made up of 89 financial services advisors, 9 vice presidents and 6 administrative assistants.

As well as teaching the participants how to forgive and the importance of forgiveness for health, the training also included emotional competence sessions on helping them to improve on aligning their thoughts, emotions and behaviour. They were also taught stress-management techniques. As part of the programme they were then given five follow-up conference calls that acted as support over the next 6–12 months.

Such was the impact of the training that for those who went through it, sales went up by 25 per cent over the next 12 months, compared with a rise of only 10 per cent for those not involved in the training. And those who received the training enjoyed 50–400 per cent increases in productivity over their colleagues.

There were, of course, health benefits too. Stress levels dropped by 23 per cent and positive emotional states rose by 20 per cent. Participants also felt improvements in the quality of their lives, physical vitality and even their feelings of anger. Quality of life rose by 10 per cent and physical vitality by 9 per cent and anger decreased by 13 per cent during the project.

Perhaps on reading this section, leaders of some corporations will learn that they can employ forgiveness training to boost profits and it will also greatly improve happiness, wellbeing and the quality of relationships within the company and with customers. And, knowing the benefits to their employees, it could even be considered an act of kindness towards them, especially if they hold the personal benefits to their employees as their primary motive for the training.

LETTING THEM OFF THE HOOK?

One of the largest obstacles to forgiveness is that we feel that we're letting offenders off the hook by forgiving them. But this is not so. Forgiveness is for *us*, not for them. When we forgive, we're being kind to *ourselves*. We don't have to forget that something happened. We are just making the choice to let it go, for the sake of our own health.

This is the sentiment of Jim La Rue, the father of Molly La Rue, a young girl who was murdered while hiking on the Appalachian Trail. In a Pennsylvania courtroom 16 years later, where the murderer was having his death sentence commuted to life in prison, Mr La Rue read out a one-page letter of forgiveness that he had written. Part of it said, 'Most people think you are forgiving the perpetrator and they're off scot-free and you get nothing. It's just the opposite. When you forgive a person, you're deciding to be freed.'[14]

It can be hard to forgive sometimes, especially when it involves someone who doesn't admit that they have done anything wrong. But when you realize that forgiveness has a lot to do with *your* choice to feel less hurt, depression or anger, it becomes less important for them to take responsibility for their actions. It's difficult to change another person, but much easier to change ourselves.

And forgiving a partner or ex-partner doesn't mean that you have to stay in an unhealthy relationship. We can acknowledge a person's behaviour but still choose to move on. Forgiving is a gift to ourselves. Sometimes it's the only way forward.

And, of course, when a perpetrator does acknowledge their actions and apologise, it can be immensely healing.

In a speech given on 13 February 2008, the Australian prime minister made a formal apology to the Aboriginal people. He spoke of an elderly women, Nana Fejo, a wonderful woman in her eighties, who was 'full of life and funny stories', but who had been forcibly taken from her mother in 1932 when she was four years old, like a large number of other children who fell victim to government policy that attempted to deal with the 'problem of the Aboriginal population'. When she was 16, she was allowed to leave the mission she had been forced into and soon discovered that her mum had died years earlier, a broken woman grieving for the children who had been stolen from her.

Decades later, the stockman who was in charge of removing Nana and other children tracked her down so that he could say sorry. And she forgave him.

Then the prime minister offered a formal apology to the Aboriginal people:

'To the stolen generations, I say the following: as Prime Minister of Australia, I am sorry. On behalf of the government of Australia, I am sorry. On behalf of the parliament of Australia, I am sorry. I offer you this apology without qualification. We apologise for the hurt, the pain and suffering that we, the parliament, have caused you by the laws that previous parliaments have enacted. We apologise for the indignity, the degradation and the humiliation these laws embodied. We offer this apology to the mothers, the fathers, the brothers, the sisters, the families and the communities whose lives were ripped apart by the actions of successive governments under successive parliaments.' [15]

The apology wasn't about forgetting the past or sweeping it under the table, but about being open and truthful about what had happened in the past so that the hurts could begin to heal and everyone could begin to take an honest step forward.

IT NEEDN'T BE ABOUT GOD

Thinking that forgiveness has to be about God is another obstacle that prevents some people from forgiving. Some non-religious people have the mistaken belief that forgiveness is about religion and by forgiving they are acknowledging the presence of a god of some kind. Though the religious aspect of forgiveness *is* highly important to some, it is not a requirement. Forgiveness is mostly achieved with no reference to religion at all.

A study by Kenneth Pargament, a psychologist at Bowling Green University, that was published in the *Journal of Clinical Psychology* showed this.[16] The study compared three groups of women. One group received religious-based counselling, another received forgiveness counselling with no mention of religion and a third group acted as a control group, so didn't receive any forgiveness training at all. The two groups that did receive training benefitted greatly. And the benefits were at the same level – it didn't matter whether the forgiveness was religiously motivated or not.

We don't have to hold grudges because we feel that forgiveness is only for 'soft' spiritual or religious people. Forgiveness is certainly not 'soft'. It is a sign of great strength and takes courage. As Gandhi said, 'The weak can never forgive. Forgiveness is the attribute of the strong.'

HEADING IN THE DIRECTION OF FORGIVING

It's often those closest to us that hurt us the most, because we have such high expectations of them. They are not supposed to hurt us.

Yet when we hold grudges, when we replay their actions over and over in our minds, it's us who suffer the most. We may believe that somehow we're hurting them too, and I guess we do hurt them if they live with us or if we see them regularly, because we give them a taste of our anger or hurt through how we treat them, or through our attitude towards them. But the cost to ourselves of festering resentment is much greater. We pay the heavier price.

Most people don't know how to forgive. Simply saying 'I forgive you' doesn't always work. Forgiveness is not a single event, it is a process. It takes time, as the feelings of hurt and anger may come up over and over again. But as we gradually forgive, we release ourselves from the thoughts that keep us tied to what happened to us. In time, hurt is replaced with peace, anger with goodwill and resentment with compassion.

The following are some tips that might help you to forgive. That is, if you have anything to forgive, of course. They are not meant as a list of steps that you have to follow in order, just as a few suggestions. Use those that work best for you.

TIPS TO HELP YOU TO FORGIVE

- Learn about how forgiveness is good for your mental and emotional health.

- Ask yourself if it's doing you any good to hold onto the grudge.

- Remind yourself that forgiveness is an act of kindness towards yourself.

- Make a determined decision to forgive.

- Take a deep breath when you catch yourself dwelling on a past hurt, and choose to move on.

- Learn to meditate.

- Pray.

- Practise a compassion meditation.

- Think of a different way of talking about the past that reflects a positive intent to move forward.

- Create a 'Forgiveness Journal' and write down your thoughts about the past, your intent to forgive and how this will make a positive difference in your life.

- Realize that you may have hurt people in the past. From this space, try to develop some empathy for and understanding of the perpetrator.

- Write about the benefits of what happened to you.

The power of the final suggestion was shown in a 2006 study at the University of Miami.[17] Researchers showed that if people wrote about the benefits of a transgression they became more forgiving. For instance, if a friend betrayed you, you might write that it helped you to see their true colours, or that it helped you to find new friends, that it even helped you to become less dependent upon that person and more independent, which was something you could now see that you had needed.

Sometimes people can even find a deeper meaning in the benefits they find. For some, they feel that the whole event happened specifically (perhaps guided by a higher source) so that they could receive that benefit and grow from it. Some then even find themselves feeling grateful to their offender.

The University of Miami study involved 304 people who were asked to write for 20 minutes. One group of them was asked to write about 'traumatic features of the most recent interpersonal transgression' they had suffered. Another group wrote about 'personal benefits resulting from the transgression' – what is known as a 'benefit-finding' condition. And a last group just wrote about a control topic that had nothing to do with the transgression.

The study found that those who wrote about the benefits of the transgression were more forgiving than the other two groups. Seeing how something might have actually benefitted us makes us more likely to want to begin the forgiveness process. It has less of a hold on us because the hurt is part lessened by the acknowledgement that we gained in some way. And we've already made a start in the forgiveness process because writing about the benefits actually encourages us to process some of what happened, as the authors of the study pointed out.

And don't forget, if all else fails, sometimes all we need is time.

Ever heard the phrase 'Time heals all wounds'? It certainly makes a difference, as many of us have already found in our life. In time, we feel differently towards someone who has offended us, even though when it first happened, and maybe even for days, weeks or months afterwards, we did not feel so forgiving.

A study at Carleton University in Ottawa, Ontario, showed that people were more likely to forgive when more time had elapsed between the event and the present. It also suggested that, culturally, our belief that time heals actually helps time to heal. In two other experiments, the scientists also showed that simply perceiving a real or hypothetical event to be further away in time increased the likelihood of forgiveness.[18]

Forgiveness really is good for our health on many levels. It helps us to let go of past hurts and the depression or anger that surrounds them. Optimism even grows out of forgiveness, for we now see a clearer path forward and feel positive about where it might lead us. Forgiveness is also good for our hearts, keeping blood pressure low and even helping our hearts recover faster from daily stresses or, in some cases, a heart attack.

When we recognize that we gain from forgiveness, it becomes an act of kindness towards ourselves. We choose to set ourselves free and move on with our life.

STORIES OF KINDNESS

'An Angel to Watch over my Car'

Having been inspired by an article I had read in the Big Issue, *I decided to organize a food collection for the Hope Centre in Northampton. It is a centre that provides hot food, clean clothing and takeaway food parcels to the homeless. A number of friends and family helped me to collect 20 large boxes of tins, packets, cereals and other non-perishable foods, which my daughter and I delivered to the centre.*

A couple of weeks later a lady called Geraldine contacted me. She told me that she had parked her car in the centre of town, not realizing that she had left her window wide open. When she returned to it an hour later she found a man guarding it. As she approached the car, the man, who called himself Stig, told her that he had been sitting on a bench near the car when he had seen a man lean in through the window and try to steal the stereo. He had chased the thief away and waited with the car until the owner returned.

It later transpired that Stig had been homeless for several months and was a regular visitor to the Hope Centre, where he had hot meals and collected a food parcel each day.

Geraldine had donated several shopping bags full of food to our collection. She had not heard of the Hope Centre before she had participated in the collection and was amazed how her kindness had returned to her so quickly! **Linzi**

CHAPTER 13

THE EVOLUTION OF KINDNESS

'When you carry out acts of kindness
you get a wonderful feeling inside. It is
as though something inside your body
responds and says, yes, this is how I ought
to feel.'
Harold Kushner

Kindness, compassion, gratitude and forgiveness are wired into
the human genome. This is why they are good for us and why not
showing them stresses our nervous systems and makes us feel
bad. We have evolved that way.

Why might this be so and how could it have happened?

We evolve when tiny mutations occur in genes when they are
passed from one generation to the next. For instance, imagine a
gene as a line of 100 light bulbs. Maybe, as they are copied, an
error takes place and a blue bulb takes the place of a red one.

This would be a mutation, called a single nucleotide polymorphism (SNP), of the gene. It is a variant of the gene.

In real terms, there are no light bulbs but a string of letters – A, C, T and G. A gene might go something like AAGTTGCCA, but a variation might cause it to read AAGTAGCCA, where an 'A' has replaced the 'T' in the fifth position.

Some gene variations are dangerous and a growing foetus aborts. Some result in disease. Most make little or no difference at all. But every now and then a mutation produces a person who is faster or slower, stronger or weaker, more resistant to a particular disease or more prone to it, or kinder or more intelligent or some other quality. The question evolution asks is, 'Does that quality give that person an advantage, a greater chance of survival?' Over the vast timescales of evolution – from millions to, at the very least, tens of thousands of years – gene variants get out into the wider population as we procreate only if they improve the chances of survival of the person with the SNP.

Over evolutionary timescales, evolution is like a race – gene versus gene for the prize of survival. To give an example, if the climate was very cold, having genes that made us sensitive to cold would be no use. Having genes that kept us warm would give us a greater chance of survival. Genes like this, which gave our ancestors advantages in the real-life race of survival, were passed to succeeding generations. Or, as the evolutionary textbooks say, nature selected those genes. This is the process of evolution by natural selection that Charles Darwin first described. It is considered one of the greatest ever contributions to science.

So, nature selects the genes that are best suited for the progression of the human species. It's not an overnight thing. But as you read this page right now, we are evolving. And over the next several thousand years we will continue to evolve as we continue to adapt to nature's environment.

The 25,000 or so genes in the current human genome were selected a long time ago because they improved the chances of survival of our ancient ancestors. And in the past it was not all about being the fittest in terms of who was the strongest, or the fastest, or the most cunning, or had the largest manhood. It had more to do with social skills. Those were the skills that helped our ancestors through the last million or so years.

WIRED TO BE CLOSE TO EACH OTHER

Our ancestors lived in a world full of predators that threatened their survival, predators that were much faster and stronger than they were and that would have won any fight. They had to band together to increase their odds of surviving. They had to cooperate. Those who formed tribes or communities, worked together to get food and protected each other from predators were more likely to survive than those who kept themselves isolated. So, genes that were suited to living and working closely together were selected by nature.

This is why we need to be close to others today. This is why, at the physiological level, social contact is better for us and social isolation is a predictor of poor health. We're wired to be together. It's why we thrive in relationships and in friendships, where we rely on each other for social support.

For groups of our ancestors to stay together, behaviour that ensured cohesion in the group was required. What type of behaviour encourages group cohesion? Love, kindness, compassion, gratitude and forgiveness! So genes that encouraged this type of behaviour were selected.

Love, kindness, compassion, gratitude and forgiveness all help the formation of strong bonds, which keep a group together. The sitcom *Friends* is a great example of this. The group of friends stayed together for 10 years through the formation of strong bonds that were built upon love, kindness, compassion, gratitude and forgiveness. Even though it was a TV show, it showed elements of real life.

WIRED FOR POSITIVE EMOTIONS

The psychologist Barbara Fredrickson, one of the leaders in the science of positive psychology, developed her 'Broaden and Build' theory of positive emotions in 1998. Put simply, the theory says that positive emotions evolved because they gave our ancestors a good chance of survival.

Briefly, positive emotions are known to broaden our awareness and encourage creativity, which helps us build skills and resources. For instance, showing kindness to someone builds a supportive friendship with them, which improves survival chances. Negative emotions, on the other hand, narrow our awareness. They are more helpful in immediate survival situations. But evolution wasn't about immediate survival every minute of the day and most of our ancestors' time would have been spent in relationship-building, where positive emotions took centre-stage.

There is growing evidence in support of this theory. Barbara Fredrickson herself conducted randomized controlled trials where participants either watched films that allowed positive emotions to arise or films that allowed fear or sadness to arise. In a subsequent test, the participants who had experienced the positive emotions showed much more creativity, inventiveness and 'big picture' focus – just the sort of abilities that would help build long-term survival skills and thereby pass the capacity for positive emotions on to succeeding generations.[1]

WIRED TO LOVE

In the modern world, couples that stay together for life share deep bonds of love for each other. No matter what troubles and challenges face them, they find a way through. In the world of our ancestors, the same thing occurred. Those whose love for each other was strong had longer-lasting relationships than those who weren't in love.

Now factor in the environment of our ancient ancestors. Getting food wasn't as simple as just going down to the shops – it had to be grown or hunted. There were many more dangers than we face today. Our ancestors lived in a much more hostile environment than we do. With the absence of laws, tribes from other lands could attack to steal food and other resources, for instance, possibly killing much of the tribe as well. And when hunting, our ancestors were exposed to other predators.

When women gave birth, the infants that had the best chance of surviving until they could take care of themselves were the ones who were most protected. Infants who had two parents to care for them fared better than those with only one parent. Having a father who stuck around served as good protection. And he was only going to stick around if he loved his partner or his child.

Similarly, parents who loved each other were more likely to stay together through the child-rearing years. So those genes that not only promoted group harmony but also made us fall in love with each other were selected and found their way into the human genome.

This is one of the reasons why love makes us healthier, because health equates to survival. This is why a loving environment promotes the growth of an infant's prefrontal cortex, making it healthier but also making the eventual adult better able to navigate the often difficult terrain of life so that its survival chances are increased.

If love weren't wired into our nervous system then it would not make us healthier, nor impact our brains in such a positive way, nor would it prolong our chances of survival.

WIRED TO FORGIVE

In the sitcom *Friends*, when Rachael couldn't forgive Ross for sleeping with another woman after they had had a serious row (from his perspective, 'We were on a break'), the group almost splintered, until they both made an effort and made up for the sake of the group. The group stayed together because of it.

Forgiveness was a necessary component of our evolution, too, because where there's no forgiveness, relationships fracture and groups fall apart. Many of us have had that experience in our lives.

Studies of primates with which we share an evolutionary history have shown that they quickly and easily reconcile after a conflict. They employ submissive displays – open hands, head down, teeth bared. Displays of this type quickly diffuse any lingering conflict. Anthropologists studying them have found that play replaces conflict often after only a few minutes. In a 1979 study of 20 chimpanzees, anthropologists observed 350 separate aggressive episodes but noted that reconciliation usually began after only one minute, and within five minutes a full 30 per cent of an individual's friendly interactions were with the individual he had just fought with.[2]

Genes that promoted the tendency to reconcile, then, were selected. And the other side of it was that our ancestors also had to accept the apologies to ensure the harmony of the group. It's the same today – groups only survive if we can accept apologies. So genes that encouraged leaders, or those high in social standing within a group, to accept apologies were also selected. Leaders who could not accept them would damage the cohesion of the group and reduce the entire group's chances of survival.

Frans de Waal, of Emory University's Yerkes Primate Center in the USA, wrote, 'In a cooperative system, it is possible that your biggest rival is someone who you will need tomorrow.'[3]

If our ancestors couldn't forgive, then they couldn't rely on that someone to help them survive.

And if forgiveness wasn't wired in us, forgiving someone wouldn't make any difference to health. But it does.

WIRED TO BE GRATEFUL

Gratitude builds relationships and strengthens bonds. The 'Big Sister' study found this. The little sisters who felt the most gratitude had the strongest relationships with their big sisters. And it is strong relationships that keep groups together.

Also, gratitude for someone's kindness often makes us want to reciprocate. And this 'paying back' also leads to stronger bonds within groups. A tapestry of more threads makes for a stronger tapestry.

In the history of our species those whose genes made them more grateful for the kindness or support of others, then, had improved chances of survival over those who didn't feel or express gratitude. On being saved from a predator or from another individual, or having food shared with them when they were hungry, showing gratefulness encouraged the strengthening of bonds.

This is clear in the present day. The field of marriage is littered with the corpses of relationships broken by one member of a partnership taking the other for granted and not being grateful for them.

The capacity to be grateful is now firmly wired into the human genome. And that's why gratitude, too, brings health benefits.

WIRED TO BE COMPASSIONATE

Kindness grows out of compassion. Charles Darwin wrote that our tendency to be sympathetic was even stronger than our instinct for survival:

'[It] will have increased through natural selection; for those communities which include the greatest number of the most sympathetic members would flourish best, and rear the greatest number of offspring.'[4]

Sympathy also builds strong relationships. Sharing the pain of another brings us closer together. Without compassion, we would see others suffer and have no motivation to help, meaning that our bonds would be weaker. In ancestral times, the groups with the fewest compassionate individuals would have a greater chance of fragmenting. Ultimately, they would rear the fewest offspring.

Compassion was especially important in rearing offspring until they could fend for themselves. Children get hurt, as any parent knows. Showing empathy and compassion for them at such times would help forge the strong bonds that would keep families, and thus groups, together.

As compassion became wired into us, the vagus nerve also evolved, which, as we have seen, is linked with compassion. Those with higher compassion and thus higher vagal tone would have fared better than those with low compassion and low vagal tone. They would have had better protection from infection and healthier hearts.

A genetic tendency to be compassionate is probably why we like those who appear vulnerable and why we strive to help them. It's probably why those who are most compassionate feel the greatest sense of kin with those who are weak or vulnerable.

Throughout history, it has often been said that compassion is for the weak. Actually, as Berkeley psychology professor Dacher Keltner writes in his book *Born to Be Good*, compassion is 'anything but weak; it fosters courageous, altruistic actions often at significant cost to the self'. Never underestimate the power of compassion. It can be a mark of courage and great strength.

WIRED TO BE KIND

When a hunter brings back an animal corpse the whole group can share in the meal – that is, if the hunter lets them. Where ancestral hunters were selfish, fights would break out over food and this would lead to groups fracturing. Harmony, on the other hand, would arise through sharing – through being kind.

And when sick or injured, our ancestors would care for each other, ensuring the strength of the bond between the sick and injured and the carer, which would add to the strength of the whole group.

Kindness built relationships in the past just as it does today. As our ancestors showed kindness to each other, not only in caring for each other and sharing food but also sharing other resources, like their homes in times of natural disasters or attack from predators or invading tribes, it forged strong bonds between them, just as such displays do today. It was the strength of these relationships forged by kindness hundreds of thousands of years ago that ensured we are here today.

So genes that encouraged kindness would have been selected because, again, they helped form strong bonds that kept groups together. This is why kindness is good for you. It's wired into you.

WHAT ABOUT SELFISH GENES?

People often talk about 'selfish genes', but this concept is sometimes misunderstood. It does not refer to us having genes that make us selfish. It refers to the indifference of the actual gene in its sole purpose of reproducing.

In his book *The Selfish Gene*, Richard Dawkins argues that a cell, in fact the entire human body, is no more than a 'survival machine' for the gene. By residing deep inside the centre of the cell, protected by the mass of the human body, genes ensure their survival. Without the cell, or the body, a gene could more easily be destroyed. The human body has actually evolved to improve the chances of survival of the gene.

The gene itself does not care about the cell or the body. It is only concerned with its own survival. So each gene is, in a sense, a selfish gene.

Ironically, these selfish genes have produced a species which is wired for kindness. But that fact doesn't automatically mean that the genes that encouraged selfishness would have died out. At times, when survival situations called for placing the self first, genes that helped that process would have been useful. Thus, these genes would have survived too and this is why, when it comes to a matter of survival, many of us have an instinct to fend for ourselves first.

I like the joke about two nature filmmakers in the African savannah who see a lion approaching. One starts to put on his trainers. The other says, 'There's no way you can outrun a lion.' And he replies, 'That doesn't matter, as long as I can outrun you.'

We have evolved the capacity for both kindness and selfishness, just as our nervous system is built for both stress and relaxation. In the autonomic nervous system, breathing in activates the sympathetic branch, which activates our inbuilt 'fight or flight' physiology, or the stress response. Breathing out, on the other hand, activates the parasympathetic branch, and the vagus nerve, and the body's 'rest and relaxation' response.

This is also why we can show compassion yet we can also show indifference, and why we can show both gratitude and ingratitude. But with the exception of a life-or-death situation, kindness is better for our mental, emotional, spiritual and physical health than selfishness. It was wired into our nervous system because it improved our chances of survival. The selfish gene produced an altruistic species.

MOLECULES OF KINDNESS

As nature selected genes that improved the chances of survival of our species, each of these genes produced a protein in the body. When a gene is activated, a protein is produced. A protein is a chain of amino acids. Think of it like a beaded necklace. Each bead is an amino acid. The string of amino acids makes it a protein.

Proteins are involved in just about every process in the body. Some are hormones, which pass information around the body, and some are enzymes, which help chemical reactions to take place in the body. Some proteins are involved in bodily movements, like actin, which is involved in the contraction of muscles, and some make up structures in the body, like collagen, which makes up connective tissue, gives skin its strength and elasticity and accounts for 25–35 per cent of all protein content in the body.

Proteins also affect our behaviour. The gene mutation (or mutations, to be more accurate, since many genes were undoubtedly
involved) that caused us to be kinder, to be close to each other,
to be compassionate, grateful and forgiving, produced proteins
that acted on the brain. One of those proteins was the hormone
oxytocin.

Oxytocin, as we have seen, is a 'kindness protein' or a 'molecule
of kindness', because its presence makes us kinder and we produce it when we're kind. It acts on the amygdala and makes us
more trusting and more generous.

The oxytocin gene was selected because it improved the chances
of survival of our ancestors by promoting group cohesion, but
also because it made our ancestors' hearts healthier and helped
keep inflammation low. Oxytocin itself, produced when the oxytocin gene was activated, also ensured that parents adored their
children and stayed around to care for them. Caring for your child
is one sure-fire way to get your genes to the next generation.
Without oxytocin, parents would not have been so attentive and
perhaps would have neglected their children.

Almost all animals need to show caring behaviour to increase the
survival chances of their offspring. It is no surprise to learn, then,
that pretty much all vertebrates have oxytocin, or an oxytocin-like
hormone that does a similar job. In fact, some research shows
that so important is oxytocin for survival that the oxytocin gene
(or its ancestor) might be as much as 500 million years old.[5] I'm
sure herds of dinosaurs that had stronger bonds were more likely
to survive than those with weaker bonds...

IT'S WRITTEN ALL OVER YOUR FACE
Some evidence for the evolution of kindness, compassion, gratitude and forgiveness lies in our facial expressions. Since all of

us share the same genetic ancestors, we would expect people all over the world to share the same types of facial expression. Even isolated cultures which have not been in contact with any 'civilized' people would be expected to share the same expressions. And this has indeed been found to be true. All cultures in the world have the same facial expressions for emotions. Happiness, for instance, universally produces a smile and sadness causes a frown.

The psychologist Paul Ekman, considered to be one of the 100 most eminent psychologists of the twentieth century and in 2009 named by *Time* magazine as one of the top 100 most influential people in the world, has studied an isolated culture of Papua New Guinea known as the Foré, a tribe which had had no prior contact with any other culture before he studied them.

Despite this, Ekman found that the Foré displayed the same facial expressions as every other culture. He did this by showing them photographs representing different emotions and inviting individuals to match the photos of facial expressions with sadness, anger, disgust, fear, surprise and happiness. It turned out that they were 80–90 per cent accurate. The Foré have the same basic facial expressions as we do in the West. The conclusion was that facial expressions, which reflect emotional state, are genetically wired and thus emotions are wired.[6]

Dacher Keltner, professor of psychology at the University of California, Berkeley, has painstakingly watched frame-by-frame videos of people experiencing these emotions. Using the facial action coding system developed by Ekman, he has provided even more evidence that emotions like compassion, embarrassment, gratefulness and even awe are reflected in our facial expressions and are thus genetic. Some of these are described in his excellent book *Born to Be Good*.[7]

Facial expressions stimulate activation of the autonomic nervous system (ANS), which is tied in with emotion. A genuine smile, for instance, signifying happiness, stimulates the parasympathetic branch of the ANS and causes our nervous system to relax. An expression of fear, however, stimulates the sympathetic branch of the ANS, increasing heart rate, blood pressure and oxygenation of the major muscles. It happens the same with all people in all cultures.

Kindness also shows up in our faces, as does compassion. We know that when watching people play the Trust Game with the sound muted, we find those who have highest vagal tone, and therefore compassion, the most trustworthy. With the sound muted, we are forming an opinion by picking up facial expressions.

Even Darwin, when he couldn't understand the languages of natives he encountered, could interpret their facial expressions. He suggested that empathy was a universal trait in his book *The Expression of the Emotions in Man and Animals*.

Other evidence comes from MRI studies of the human brain taken while a person is watching another person suffer. The brain areas activated show that we empathize with the pain of another. This capacity is present from the moment we are born, suggesting the brain circuits involved are genetic. In infants, it is known as emotional contagion – emotions are contagious.

In a 2009 study of emotional contagion and empathy, emotional contagion was referred to as 'primitive empathy'.[8] That's because emotional contagion is a primitive, automatic response in the brain when we become aware of the suffering of another. It is well known, for instance, that a baby will start crying when it hears the cries of another baby. And this occurs before its brain has even developed the capacity to know itself as separate from others. Emotional contagion, from which kindness eventually grows, is completely involuntary. It is wired into the brain.

Another example of this was shown in 2006 by scientists at University College London.[9] When participants in the study were shown photographs of sad faces with small pupil sizes, their own pupils reduced in size. And their pupil sizes also mirrored the pupil size of people they observed. MRI brain scans taken while this was happening revealed the Edinger-Westphal nucleus in the brainstem was activated, the region that controls pupil size. The point here is that it is believed that pupil size is linked with empathy and may even be a precursor to it.

EVIDENCE OF KINDNESS

Genetics research now confirms that some of our kind behaviour is indeed linked with our genes. A seminal 2007 study led by scientists at the Hebrew University of Jerusalem found that variations in one particular gene made people either more or less generous. The gene was for the receptor of a neuropeptide called vasopressin.

Vasopressin is very similar to oxytocin. Both have nine amino acids, differ only in two amino acids and share a very similar evolutionary history, having, it is believed, evolved from the same precursor gene around 500 million years ago. Just like oxytocin, vasopressin is involved in social behaviour. It is involved in water homeostasis too and is often given to cause water retention. Children who wet the bed stop when given vasopressin.

The scientists studied the gene that produces the vasopressin receptor, known as AVPR1a, and homed in on a section of it known as the 'promoter' region, which is repeated several times throughout the gene. More repeats equal a longer promoter region. Then they compared the results of the Dictator Game (another economics game) with the number of repeats.

In the study, the game was played by 203 male and female university students. It is similar to the Ultimatum Game that we learned about earlier, only the person receiving the funds must accept whichever sum is given. It is considered a test of altruism because it involves real money and the person giving doesn't have to give anything at all. It has been referred to as a 'put your money where your mouth is' game because what you give you don't get back, and it is done anonymously so no one gets to meet the player they are paired with.

The scientists found that the length of the promoter region on the vasopressin receptor, AVPR1a, was related to how much the dictators gave to the second player. Those who had longest promoter regions in the gene were found to be most generous. In fact, they were around 50 per cent more likely to give money away than those without the variant. Short promoter regions equated to more selfish behaviour – less giving.[10]

Longer promoter regions mean that vasopressin acts more strongly on brain cells because it determines how tightly it binds to the AVPR1a receptor. And it binds in reward regions of the brain, which therefore gives us a positive feeling when we act kindly.

The study showed that we are wired for kindness because we have genes that make us kind and that variations in specific genes affect how kind we are.

In a second study, performed in 2009 by the same research team, the gene for the oxytocin receptor was also found to influence kind behaviour.[11]

Instead of examining the promoter region of the gene, this time the scientists studied 15 individual variations in the gene, single nucleotide polymorphisms (SNPs), as we learned at the start of the chapter, or 'snips' for short. Using another sample of 203 students and again playing the Dictator Game, they found an association between three of the snips and prosocial behaviour, which is 'voluntary behaviour connected with the intent of benefitting others'.

Once again, the study showed that kindness is wired. If it were not, then variations in the vasopressin or oxytocin receptor genes would have no effect on kind behaviour.

The oxytocin receptor gene has even now been linked with empathy. In 2009 research, scientists at Oregon State University and the University of California at Berkeley discovered that variations of the oxytocin receptor gene were also related to how empathetic a person was. Using a sample of 200 college students, the scientists found that having a specific variant of the gene known as GG generally meant a person would show more empathy.[12]

An earlier study, published in 2005 by scientists at the Hebrew University in Jerusalem and Herzog Memorial Hospital in Jerusalem, homed in on another gene. Examining the responses given by 354 families to questionnaires about selflessness, they found that those who showed more selflessness had specific SNPs of the gene for the dopamine receptor on brain cells, which can vary in the number of repeats, producing shorter or longer forms of the gene. It is believed that the variants in kinder people bind dopamine more tightly and lead to a greater positive feeling when those people do something good.[13]

Essentially, kindness is our nature. Non-genetic studies that employ economic games have also confirmed it. In the Ultimatum Game, where one player is given $10 and has to give some to another player who can either accept or reject it, if our nature were selfish then most people would give as little as possible, but in a study conducted over 12 different cultures, 71 per cent of those giving the money offered 40–50 per cent of it.[14] They didn't need to give that much away, but an inbuilt sense of fairness prompted them to be generous.

Some people did keep most of the money, of course, but most shared it. Many, in fact, would give most of it away, keeping only what they believed they needed, to ensure that others had as much as they needed too. I'm sure you know people who would fit this category.

In another study that pitted our true nature against itself, participants had to watch others taking part in a memory test. When a person made a mistake they would receive a painful electric shock. But, unknown to the participants, those receiving the shocks were in on the experiment and faking the pain. As the shocks became more frequent and 'obviously' more painful, the participants were given the opportunity to take some of them on behalf of the other people.

The experiment was designed to determine whether participants would take the selfish or the compassionate route. No one would ever have to know if they walked away or not. But the compassionate route won. People were more inclined to take a shock for someone else than not, even though no one would know what they did. It was an anonymous act of compassion.[15]

★★★★★

So we're wired to be kind, compassionate, grateful and forgiving. The theory of evolution by natural selection shows how it could have happened and recent genetic studies have now identified some of the genes that influence kind behaviour. Of course we have the capacity to be selfish too, but when it comes down to it most of us tend to be kind.

As Dr Wayne W. Dyer said, 'Kindness is not just something that you do. It's something that you are.'

Selfishness, then, is perhaps something that we have had to learn, a product of our social and cultural environment and, for many, perhaps a product of an underdeveloped prefrontal cortex. But kindness is better for us. So many studies now show that we are at our healthiest when we are being kind, or compassionate, or grateful, or forgiving. And that includes being kind to ourselves.

STORIES OF KINDNESS

Learning to Smile Again

I was having the worst day. I was stressed out, preparing for a really important meeting about a contract that I felt I really needed to win to keep my job. I hadn't been long in the job and all my hours and energy were going into impressing my boss.

Things hadn't been going well so far: I'd failed to bring in business that I had promised my boss at interview that I could 'guarantee'. And this morning I had just been rejected by yet another 'guaranteed' client. It just felt as though the whole world was against me.

I was walking through the rat race that is London, feeling sorry for myself, feeling that everyone was out for themselves. People were elbowing past me to get to the tube faster, so they'd get a seat, or at least just squeeze on.

I was rushing to a meeting that I was already late for and absolutely had to get that tube. But just as I was about to get on it, I found that I couldn't. It was jam-packed. Full to the brim. The doors then started to close. Desperately, I pleaded for someone to get off. I so needed to make that meeting.

Just as the doors were closing, a girl in her twenties put her bag in between the doors, which re-opened them. She got out and told me to take her place. She was in no hurry. Stunned, as I didn't think anyone would do such a kind thing, I thanked her numbly and, very humbly, got on.

As the doors closed and the train pulled away, I looked at the girl and smiled. It was the first time I had smiled all week. I had forgotten what it felt like. The muscles in my face felt relieved. I had a lump in my throat. Tears welled up in my eyes. Suddenly, the meeting just didn't seem so important any more. Instead, life did. It made me realize that if a kind act could make me feel this good, then that is what would bring me happiness on a daily basis, not a contract that could bring me a financial bonus.

I ended up getting to the meeting a minute late. I apologized, but I was calm. Extremely calm – and happy. I got the contract. I kept my job. I ended up with the best of both worlds, but I can honestly say that if I had managed to squeeze into the tube in the first place and had been bang on time, with the stress showing on my face and my nervousness about the outcome, I really don't think I would have got it.

That experience has reminded me to show kindness whenever I possibly can, because you just never know the impact it may have. **Rashida**

CHAPTER 14

KINDNESS TOWARDS OURSELVES

'Thousands of candles can be lit from a single candle, and the life of the candle will not be shortened. Happiness never decreases by being shared.'

Buddha

One thing that we haven't discussed so far, and it wouldn't be right to end without it, is being kind to ourselves.

This is something that most of us completely miss, but it is so important. There are so many benefits to being kind to others but, as we learned in the first chapter, it is possible to wear ourselves out. Sometimes, just a little time out can be a tonic for the soul, picking us up when we feel frazzled by the stresses and strains of our daily lives.

Philo of Alexandria wrote, 'Be kind, for everyone you meet is fighting a hard battle.' What we forget is that this applies to us too. Many of us are fighting a hard battle and a little kindness towards ourselves goes a long way. This might just mean having a day or even a few hours to ourselves. Have you ever noticed that no matter how busy you get, if someone really needs your time you'll find a space in your schedule? Well, we need to find time in our schedules for ourselves.

Sometimes I block out a morning in my diary and write, 'Meeting with Self'. This is me-time. I don't always do anything of significance with it. For me, this is just time when I try not to think. For you, it might be a time when you want to shop, or go for a walk, or a swim, or visit the gym, or see a loved one, or even just sit in the park, or when you get out your journal and write what's in your heart. But whatever you do, when you are taking me-time, you are being kind to yourself because you are taking time for yourself.

As we learned earlier, forgiveness can also be an act of kindness towards ourselves. In forgiving, we are the ones benefitting most. Doing a kind of gratitude exercise on ourselves can also give us a warm feeling. Make a list of your best qualities and read it often. OK, for some people this can be tough, but work at it.

As children, we are only too happy to tell others what we're good at, but as adults we seem to think there's something wrong in it. I remember when my nephew Jake was about three years old. He was cycling around on a little plastic tractor and I was taken by the speed he was pedalling but also by how he was skilfully steering around objects at speed, just narrowly missing them and then ending with a skid. When he pulled up beside me, I remember saying, 'You're amazing, Jake,' to which he enthusiastically replied, 'I know. I am amazing, eh?'

Not being able to acknowledge our good points can be a sign that we lack compassion for ourselves, something that is called *self-compassion*.

SELF-COMPASSION

Self-compassion is defined as 'being open to and moved by one's own suffering, experiencing feelings of caring and kindness toward oneself, taking an understanding, non-judgemental attitude toward one's inadequacies and failures, and recognizing that one's experience is part of the common human experience'. Phew. But we really can be our own worst enemies, beating ourselves up not only for things that have happened in the past but also for how we've dealt with situations. We often treat ourselves worse than we treat others.

Self-compassion is not to be confused with self-esteem. Self-esteem is having positive feelings about ourselves and feeling valued by other people. Self-compassion, on the other hand, is *caring* for ourselves. People who are self-compassionate also have high self-esteem but it's not always true the other way around.

Self-compassion shows a lack of ego or self-inflated thought. Some people with high self-esteem, on the other hand, do show a tendency to have something of an ego. Many with high self-esteem are genuinely self-compassionate and have positive feelings about themselves. But some are narcissistic, and it's on the increase.

A 2006 study that examined the questionnaire responses of 16,475 college students between 1982 and 2006 found that narcissism had greatly increased over the previous 24 years.[1] That's not so good for us. Although the students were considerably more confident and assertive in 2006 than they were in 1982, and had much greater self-belief regarding achieving their dreams, which is testimony to the self-help movement, they were also 30 per cent more narcissistic, more self-centred and more depressed.

Perhaps all we really need to do now is tweak the idea of self-esteem and move towards self-compassion instead. This will eventually breed greater compassion for all and allow kindness to flower in our hearts.

Self-compassion is very important not only because it encourages us to be kinder to ourselves but because some people are harsh on themselves because of a mistaken belief that if they celebrate themselves or if they are kind to themselves it is a form of narcissism or big-headedness. This is close to my own heart because through my teenage years I was criticized and made fun of for being bigheaded. My intent was never ever to try to make anyone else small but to celebrate my accomplishments and capabilities. After many years of this and a year of repetitive bullying in my final school year, I left at 17 years of age and went to university with a very much eroded sense of self-worth which took me years to overcome.

The blurred lines in most people's minds between self-compassion and self-esteem cause many to put themselves down so as never to be seen to be trying to be better than others. I grew up in a small village in central Scotland where this was obvious to me. I witnessed much kindness, which was inspiring to me, but many people in the village had a low opinion of themselves, including those close to me. I feel that this was partly because they didn't ever want to be seen to be trying to appear better than others. This need to be valued equally was ingrained in the culture of the area and I am proud to come from a place where equality in how we are valued and should be treated is so important. But low self-compassion has now been linked with depression and poor psychological wellbeing. We all need to have some self-compassion.

Having self-compassion is especially important when we fail at things in life, which we all do at some stage. It is part of normal human experience. But people who are self-compassionate are better able to recover from disappointments and find the silver lining. They are better able to find a positive way of interpreting difficult experiences and finding something of value in them.

This was shown in some research published in 2005 in the journal *Self and Identity*. Students who had received an unsatisfactory mid-term grade but who scored high on self-compassion were more accepting than those low in self-compassion. They even found a way to see it in a positive light. Those low in self-compassion, on the other hand, experienced more negative emotions.[2]

In a 2007 study published in the *Journal of Personality and Social Psychology*, self-compassion was investigated in a variety of different situations.[3] In one part of the study, participants were asked to list the worst things that had happened to them on four occasions during a 20-day period. Those who scored high on self-compassion were much kinder to themselves and tried to make themselves feel better than those low on the scale. They kept the situation more in perspective. They recognized that everyone had problems and that theirs were no worse than anyone else's. People low on self-compassion, on the other hand, had the opposite perception. They considered that their problems were bigger than everyone else's, that they were worse off and more screwed up than other people and that they were somehow singled out for misfortune.

In another part of the study, self-compassionate people were found to be calmer and less likely to make situations a catastrophe (make a mountain out of a molehill, so to speak) and also less likely to take things personally. Those low on self-compassion were more likely to feel overwhelmed with negativity when asked to recall past failures, losses or rejections that had caused them to feel bad at the time. Self-compassionate people were better able to acknowledge the role they had played in these situations.

Overall, studies show that people high in self-compassion react with greater calmness of mind when faced with difficult situations than people with low self-compassion. Self-compassion seems to protect us from some of life's challenges, past and present, buffering us from the pain and helping us to see more clearly a way forward.

It is a mark of kindness to the self to be self-compassionate. Start today by showing yourself more care, attention and forgiveness, and by treating yourself.

KINDNESS IS THE WAY

Kindness to yourself is, then, perhaps the most important form of kindness. It's a necessary starting-point for many who need to reorganize their focus in life. It is not being narcissistic. It does not arise from an inflated sense of self-importance and is not to the detriment of anyone else. It is not saying, 'I am *more* important than you,' it is saying, 'I am *as* important as you.' It is simply caring for your needs. Because we all have needs that we shouldn't ignore.

And when we take care of ourselves, we begin to expand. We have more energy, and confidence, and conviction, and wisdom, and clarity regarding our future. Kindness for others becomes more natural then, and effortless. Compassion needs no thought. Gratitude flows out of us continually. And the hurts of the past fade away.

And as you expand, you touch many others along the way through life. People stop and wonder what it is that you do that makes you so full. And you don't have to tell them anything. All you need to do is be yourself and they will see for themselves. Because kindness is your way.

I believe that all of life is interconnected. We cannot disentangle ourselves from the world. All that we do, all that we are, contributes to the whole. As we learn to be kind to ourselves and others, we benefit the whole.

Thus, in our own small but significant way, we add a little more completeness to the picture, and the heart of the world smiles.

IN CLOSING

We all know that kindness is good for those who receive it. But I hope you have now learned that kindness is good for the giver too. Acts of kindness make us happier and healthier, they relieve the symptoms of depression and they even help us live longer, healthier lives.

When we show kindness, oxytocin flows in our brains and bodies. In the brain, it reduces anxiety about being betrayed or taken advantage of, encouraging us to be more trusting. This is a win-win scenario for everyone. And in the body, oxytocin is cardioprotective. It protects us from hardening of the arteries, it dilates our blood vessels, reduces blood pressure, encourages wound healing, helps in the construction of foetal hearts and may even help in the regeneration of the heart following damage.

It is produced when we connect with each other and a large number of studies now show that good relationships are good for our health. In fact, they are cardioprotective, probably because they produce oxytocin. People in healthy relationships are at lower risk of heart disease than people who are single. Being around people is also good for us. So get good at making friends and be there for them when they need it. Social isolation is also associated with a greater risk of heart disease.

Kindness is actually of paramount importance for us even as babies. When a baby is born, the love, care, joy, play, compassion, tenderness and responsiveness of the primary caregiver mould the structure of its brain. The orbitofrontal cortex is formed almost entirely after birth and this is the part that is responsible for helping a growing child to become emotionally well-adjusted and able to make responsible, mature choices. We all have a responsibility to help the children of the world develop through showing them great love and care.

Gratitude is another practice that can make a difference in our lives. It is an expression of kindness because in counting our blessings we are saying thank you to someone or to the world or even to God. Gratitude can make us happier, alleviate symptoms of depression and even help us get a good night's sleep. It also helps build and strengthen relationships.

Forgiveness, too, is good for us. It is a process that helps us to get over emotional pain. It also reduces anger and depression. It is something that we do for ourselves, not for the offender. And it can leave us with a greater sense of optimism and hope for the future.

Empathy is often the starting-point for kindness. We sense and share another's pain, compassion arises and we begin to wish them free of their pain, and then we are motivated to do something kind to help.

Compassion also happens to be good for us. It strengthens the immune system. It even buffers the effects of stress and can help us live longer.

Scientists now believe that ageing is actually like a disease, that the possible lifespan of the human body far exceeds what we currently live to. They believe that inflammation is a primary cause of ageing and are excited at the prospect of finding a new anti-inflammatory drug that can combat it.

But the drug, as we now know, isn't a drug but a nerve. The vagus nerve is the primary brake on inflammation in the body. It stops the collateral damage caused by the dripping tap of inflammation.

We can stimulate the vagus nerve through kindness and compassion. Kindness produces oxytocin that tickles the vagus nerve in the brain and reduces inflammation throughout the body. Compassion also stimulates the vagus nerve. So does the deep breathing that we do in meditation.

We have far more control, then, over the ageing process than we think. We have known for a while that having a healthy diet and exercising can prolong our lives. Evidence that has emerged recently shows that having a positive attitude also makes us live longer. But now we must add kindness and compassion to the lifespan equation. No longer can we just think of kindness as something that can benefit others. At the deepest biological level in the body, it benefits us too.

And this is, as we know, because we're wired for kindness. Evolution has set up the human body to be at its best, its healthiest, when we're being kind, compassionate, grateful and forgiving, and when we're around friends and loved ones. Evolution has always been about survival. Kindness, compassion, gratitude, forgiveness and having friends and loved ones to share with and depend upon are what got our ancestors through perilous times. We are here today because our ancestors were kind to each other. And we will be here tomorrow, and a little bit longer, if we are kind today.

So kindness is highly beneficial to us, but it is not just for us. It is for those we help too. In fact our primary motivation, when we are being kind, is to help.

At heart, we are good people. We have evolved that way. And when we express our goodness by being kind, everyone around us benefits.

THE 21-DAY KINDNESS CHALLENGE

We know that kindness is good for us. It's also good for others. A simple act can bring a smile to a person's face for a whole day. It can be just the tonic for them.

We can never know how far an act of kindness can travel. It might alter someone's behaviour, causing them to be softer or gentler through the rest of the day. Without it, who knows? Maybe they would have caused someone pain.

And kindness begets kindness. As Amelia Earhart said,

'No kind action ever stops with itself. One kind action leads to another. Good example is followed. A single act of kindness throws out roots in all directions, and the roots spring up and make new trees. The greatest work that kindness does to others is that it makes them kind themselves.'[1]

My challenge to you is to do an act of kindness every day for 21 days.

Where do you start? First, get a really nice journal – something that feels soft and special, that feels appropriate for what you're filling it with.

Then, as you carry out your acts of kindness over the next 21 days, record what you did and how it made you feel. Note how it affected the person, or people, you were kind to – that's if you know, of course. And try to vary your acts so you're not doing the same thing every day.

I would also like you to carry out some acts of kindness anonymously and record how these make you feel. The rule here is that no one can ever know that it was you who was kind. See how you get on!

THREE ACTS OF KINDNESS A DAY

Once you've done the 21-day challenge, keep up the kindness whenever an opportunity arises. You'll soon notice a difference in how you feel.

But in addition, pick one day of the week – many people like to make it Friday – and carry out three acts of kindness on that day. Make this a habit. Let this be your kindness day. Maybe your boss could even make it a weekly theme, or if you're the boss then you could take the initiative.

Once again, try to vary your acts of kindness. Writing thank-you cards all the time is good, for example, but you will get more out of doing other things too.

A FEW IDEAS FOR SCHOOLTEACHERS

If children are educated about the importance of kindness early enough then it becomes a habit for them, a way of life. And they are the leaders of the next generation. So, if we educate them early enough then we might just see a better world emerge.

Here are a few ideas:

- Schoolteachers could make kindness games a theme for a regular lesson. Children could be encouraged to write one nice thing about each member of the class and then the teacher could make up each person's list of nice things.

  There could be a special day where each person is presented with a scroll containing all the nice things written about them.

- Children could also be encouraged to do good turns when opportunities arise. In a more structured approach, schools could create volunteer programmes where children are taken out for two hours a week to help out in, say, hospitals or hospices, where they can visit sick or elderly people. Older children could be invited to help teach children with learning difficulties.

- Children could be taught the benefits of kindness to themselves and others using crafts, paints and colours.

- Why not start a kindness box? Invite the students to write down all the kind things they do and post them in the box. At the end of each week or month, the class can all read them together.

- Start a kindness week in school, where all the students are encouraged to do random acts of kindness for a full week. At the end, ask the students to write an essay describing what they did, how they felt, how their kindness helped others and what kindness means to them. Some high schools call these weeks 'RAK week', meaning 'Random Acts of Kindness week'.

- Start a Kindness Club, where students can meet regularly and coordinate volunteer efforts.

- Ask students to collect kindness quotations and then together make a large poster for the wall with art combined with the quotations.

FIFTY ACTS OF KINDNESS

And finally, just to get you started, here is a list of 50 suggestions for acts of kindness:

1. Write a thank-you card to someone.

2. Offer to carry an elderly person's shopping.

3. Allow someone in front of you in the supermarket queue.

4. Give someone a compliment.

5. Buy an extra parking ticket and leave it on the parking meter for the next person to find.

6. Pay for an extra pair of cinema tickets and ask the server to give them to someone they feel would appreciate them.

7. Leave £20 at the till of a coffee shop and ask the manager to use it to pay for everyone's coffees until it is used up.

8. Tell someone in a shop or restaurant that they're doing a great job.

9. When someone cuts you up on the road, smile and wave them on.

10. Send a card to a schoolteacher or university professor you once had and tell them how much they influenced your life.

11. Buy some food for a homeless person.

12. Use an online supermarket service and send a box of food to a family you know could use it.

13. Join a charity as a regular volunteer.

14. Offer to look after a friend or family member's children for a few hours.

15. Phone someone up on their birthday and sing, 'Happy Birthday' down the phone line to them.

16. Offer your seat on the bus or train to an elderly person.

17. Be a friend to someone in need.

18. Make a donation to a charity.

19. Sponsor a child.

20. Foster or adopt a child from an orphanage.

21. Buy a large box of cakes and pastries and give them out on the street.

22. Take out an advert in a newspaper wishing everyone a nice day.

23. Give your loved one breakfast in bed.

24. Buy a gift for someone.

25. Buy lunch or dinner for someone who is short of money.

26. If someone is giving out leaflets on the street, take one, smile and thank them for offering it to you. Make a point of reading it.

27. If you are ever given too much change, take it back to the shop.

28. Give blood.

29. Write a letter of gratitude to someone who has influenced your life, hand-deliver it and read it out to them.

30. If you're getting a coffee for yourself in the office, offer to get one for your colleagues, or just surprise someone with a coffee on your return.

31. Send chocolates at Christmas to a company that has provided you with good service.

32. Send flowers to an elderly person.

33. Visit an elderly person and listen to their stories.

34. Find out what a loved one or friend really wants and provide it for them.

35. Buy a book for someone.

36. Tell someone they look great.

37. Throw a party for someone who deserves some appreciation.

38. Offer to tidy an elderly neighbour's garden.

39. Offer to do some shopping for someone who's not able to do it for themselves.

40. Take someone on a night out.

41. When a new person joins the company you work for or moves into your street, make them feel welcome by taking them for lunch.

42. Hold a door open for someone.

43. Slip some money into the purse or pocket of someone who needs it so that when they find it they think they must have misplaced it.

44. Write a poem or song for someone.

45. Search out inspirational or funny videos on YouTube, or other inspirational or funny material, and send it to someone who needs it.

46. Pay a kindness forward. If someone does something kind for you, do something kind for someone else, to carry the kindness forward.

47. Do a chore for someone that you know they hate doing.

48. Give someone a hug for no reason.

49. Write a thank-you card to a teacher or university professor and thank them for an inspiring or informative lesson.

50. Take a loaf of bread to a pond and feed the ducks.

CHAPTER 1: KINDNESS IS THE BEST MEDICINE

1. *For the study of the 122 people given a flower, see* K. Baskerville, K. Johnson, E. Monk-Turner, Q. Slone, H. Standley, S. Stansbury, M. Williams and J. Young, 'Reactions to random acts of kindness', *Science* 37(2), 2000, 293–8

2. *For the study where kindness trumped good looks and financial prospects, see* D. M. Buss, 'Sex differences in human mate preference: evolutionary hypothesis tested in 37 countries', *Behavioral and Brain Sciences* 12, 1989, 1–49; *also* Dacher Keltner, *Born to Be Good: The Science of a Meaningful Life*, Norton, New York, 2009. In this book, Professor Keltner has extracted the relevant information from the 1989 paper and represented it. I used his presentation of the stats as my main source, but cross-checked with the source paper.

3. *For the gossip studies, see* Keltner, ibid.

4. *For information on the 'Foresight' project, visit:* http://www.foresight.gov.uk (accessed 22 September 2009)

5. *For the 2008 study linking giving money away with happiness, see* E. W. Dunn, L. Aknin and M. I. Norton, 'Spending money on others promotes happiness', *Science* 319, 2008, 1,687–8

6. *For the study showing the effects of five acts of kindness a day, see* S. Lyubomirsky, C. Tkach and K. M. Sheldon, 'Pursuing sustained happiness through random acts of kindness and counting one's blessings: tests of two six-week interventions', Department of Psychology, University of California, Riverside, unpublished data, 2004

7. *For the 'very happy' study involving 119 Japanese women, see* K. Otake, S. Shimai, J. Tanaka-Matsumi, K. Otsui and B. Fredrickson, 'Happy people become happier through kindness: a counting kindness intervention', *Journal of Happiness Studies* 7(3), 2006, 361–75

8. Allan Luks, *The Healing Power of Doing Good*, iUniverse.com, Lincoln, 1991

9. *For the 2001 study linking regular volunteering with six aspects of well-being, see* P. A. Thoits and L. N. Hewitt, 'Volunteer work and well-being', *Journal of Health and Social Behaviour* 42(2), 2001, 115–31

10. *For the 2008 study comparing 'Volunteering my time' etc. with 'Went to a big party' behaviour, see* M. F. Steger, T. B. Kashdan and S. Oishi, 'Being good by doing good: daily eudaimonic activity and well-being', *Journal of Research in Personality* 42, 2008, 22–42

11. *For the 16-year study of the earnings of college students, see* Robert A. Emmons, *Thanks*, Houghton Mifflin Company, New York, 2007

12. *For a number of studies linking happiness with better health, see* Martin E. P. Seligman, *Authentic Happiness*, Nicholas Brealey, Boston, 2003

13. *For information on moral treatment as a historical treatment for depression, see* T. Taubes, 'Healthy avenues of the mind: psychological theory building and the influence of religion during the era of moral treatment', *American Journal of Psychiatry* 155, 1998, 1,001–8

14. *For the 2003 University of Texas study linking volunteering and reduced depression, see* M. A. Musick and J. Wilson, 'Volunteering and depression: the role of psychological and

social resources in different age groups', *Social Science and Medicine* 56(2), 2003, 259–69

15. *For the 2004 University of Wisconsin study linking volunteering and reduced depression, see* E. A. Greenfield and N. F. Marks, 'Formal volunteering as a protective factor for older adults' psychological well-being', *Journal of Gerontology Series B, Psychological Sciences and Social Sciences* 59(5), 2004, S258–64

16. *For the 2004 study linking altruism and happiness, see* E. Kahana, K. Feldman, C. Fechner, E. Midlarsky and B. Kahana, 'Altruism and volunteering: effects on psychological well-being in the old-old', Paper presented at the Gerontological Society of America Meetings, Washington, DC, 2004

17. *For the 1981 study comparing people aged over 65 who volunteer with those who don't, see* K. I. Hunter and M. W. Linn, 'Psychosocial differences between elderly volunteers and non-volunteers', *International Journal of Aging and Human Development* 12(3), 1980–81, 205–13

18. *For the 1973 study where black inner-city teenagers tutored fourth- and fifth-grade children, see* G. A. Rogeness and R. A. Bednar, 'Teenage helper: a role in community mental health', *American Journal of Psychiatry* 130, 1973, 933–6

19. *For the 'Teen Outreach' study, see* J. P. Allen, S. Philliber, S. Herrling and G. P. Kuperminc, 'Preventing teen pregnancy and academic failure: experimental evaluation of a developmentally based approach', *Child Development* 64(4), 1997, 729–42

20. *For the 2004 study where alcoholics helped other alcoholics abstain, see* M. E. Pagano, K. B. Friend, J. S. Tonigan and R. L. Stout, 'Helping other alcoholics in Alcoholics Anonymous and drinking outcomes: findings from project match', *Journal of Studies on Alcohol* 65(6), 2004, 766–73

21. *For the 2002 study showing the back pain-relieving effects of helping others, see* P. Arnstein, M. Vidal, C. Wells-Federman, B. Morgan and M. Caudill, 'From chronic pain patient to peer: benefits and risks of volunteering', *Pain Management Nursing* 3(3), 2002, 94–103

22. *Allan Luks' research can be found in* Allan Luks, *The Healing Power of Doing Good*, iUniverse.com, Lincoln, 1991

23. *For the 2008 Australian National University study about number of hours people volunteered, see* T. D. Windsor, K. J. Anstey and B. Rodgers, 'Volunteering and psychological well-being among young-old adults: how much is too much?', *Gerontologist* 48(1), 2008, 59–70

24. *For the study of the 2,016 church congregation members, see* C. Schwartz, J. B. Meisenhelder, Y. Ma and G. Reed, 'Altruistic social interest behaviours are associated with better mental health', *Psychosomatic Medicine* 65, 2003, 778–85

25. *For the 1988 Harvard study of students watching a Mother Teresa video, see* D. C. McClelland and C. Kirshnit, 'The effect of motivational arousal through films on salivary immunoglobulin A', *Psychology and Health* 2(1), 1988, 31–52

26. *For the study of children watching the bowling video, see* Dacher Keltner, *Born to Be Good: The Science of a Meaningful Life*, Norton, New York, 2009

27. *For the study of children watching the Lassie movie, see* ibid.

28. *For the 1999 study of volunteering reducing mortality rate, see* D. Oman, C. E. Thoresen and K. McMahon, 'Volunteerism and mortality among the community dwelling elderly', *Journal of Health Psychology* 4(3), 1999, 301–16

29. *For the 2005 study linking volunteer habits with mortality rate, see* A. H. S. Harris and C. E. Thoresen, 'Volunteering is

associated with delayed mortality in older people: analysis of the longitudinal study of aging', *Journal of Health Psychology* 10(6), 2005, 739–52

30. *For the study linking spiritual and religious beliefs with HIV/AIDS survival, see* G. Ironson, G. F. Solomon, E. G. Balbin, C. O'Cleirigh, A. George, M. Kumar, D. Larson and T. E. Woods, 'The Ironson-Woods spirituality/religiosity index is associated with long survival, health behaviours, less distress, and low cortisol in people with HIV/AIDS', *Annals of Behavioural Medicine* 24(1), 2002, 34–48

31. *For the study where optimists were found to live 7.5 years longer than pessimists, see* B. R. Levy, M. D. Slade, S. R. Kunkel and S. V. Kasl, 'Longevity increased by positive self-perceptions of ageing', *Journal of Personality and Social Psychology* 83(2), 2002, 261–70

32. *For the 2004 study linking telomere length with chronic stress of looking after chronically ill children, see* E. S. Epel, E. H. Blackburn, J. Lin, F. S. Dhabhar, N. E. Adler, J. D. Morrow and R. M. Cawthorn, 'Accelerated telomere shortening in response to life stress', *Proceedings of the National Academy of Sciences USA* 101, 2004, 17,312–15

33. *For the 2007 NIH study linking telomere shortening with the chronic stress of looking after Alzheimer's patients, see* A. K. Damjanovic, Y. Yang, R. Glaser, J. Kiecolt-Glaser, H. Nguyen, B. Laskowski, Y. Zou, D. Q. Beversdorf and N-P. Weng, 'Accelerated telomere erosion is associated with a declining immune function of caregivers of Alzheimer's disease patients', *Journal of Immunology* 179(6), 2007, 4,249–54

34. *For the 2006 study linking discrimination with coronary artery calcification, see* T. T. Lewis, S. A. Everson-Rose, L. H. Powell, K. A. Mathews, C. Brown, K. Karavolos, K. Sutton-Tyrell, E. Jacobs and D. Wesley, 'Chronic exposure to everyday discrimination

and coronary artery calcification in African-American women: the SWAN heart study', *Psychosomatic Medicine* 68, 2006, 362–8

35. *For the 2009 study linking discrimination with increased blood pressure, see* T. T. Lewis, L. L. Barnes, J. L. Bienias, D. T. Lackland, D. A. Evans and C. F. Mendes de Leon, 'Perceived discrimination and blood pressure in older African American and white adults', *Journal of Gerontology Series A: Biological Sciences and Medical Sciences* 64A(9), 2009, 1,002–8

36. *For the 2008 loving-kindness meditation study, see* B. Fredrickson, M. Cohn, K. A. Coffey, J. Pek and S. M. Finkel, 'Open hearts build lives: positive emotions, induced through loving-kindness meditation, build consequential personal resources', *Journal of Personality and Social Psychology* 95(5), 2008, 1,045–62

37. *For the 2005 study of loving-kindness meditation for chronic low back pain, see* J. W. Carson, F. J. Keefe, T. R. Lynch, K. M. Carson, V. Goli, A-M. Fras, S. R. Thorp, 'Loving-kindness meditation for chronic low back pain', *Journal of Holistic Nursing* 23(3), 287–304

38. *For references to loving-kindness meditation helping to build relationships, see* T. G. Plante and C. E. Thorensen, *Spirit, Science, and Health: How the Spiritual Mind Fuels Physical Wellness*, Praeger Publishers, Westport, 2007

CHAPTER 2: 'I FEEL FOR YOU': THE POWER OF COMPASSION

1. *For some studies linking prefrontal cortex thickness with meditation, see* David R. Hamilton, PhD, *How Your Mind Can Heal Your Body*, Hay House, 2008; *also* S. W. Lazar, C. E. Kerr, R. H. Wasserman, J. R. Gray, D. N. Greve, *et al.*, 'Meditation experience is associated with increased cortical thickness', *Neuroreport* 16, 2005, 1,893–7

2. *For a study on mirror neurons and stroke rehabilitation, see* D. Ertelt, S. Small, A. Solodkin, C. Dettmers, A. McNamara, F. Binkofski and G. Buccino, 'Action observation has a positive impact on rehabilitation of motor deficits after stroke', *Neuroimage* 36(Suppl. 2), 2007, T164–73

3. T. Singer and C. Lamm, 'The social neuroscience of empathy', *Annals of the New York Academy of Sciences* 1,156, 2009, 81–96

4. *For general information on the neural correlates of empathy, see:* G. Hein and T. Singer, 'I feel how you feel but not always: the empathetic brain and its modulation', *Current Opinion in Neurobiology* 18, 2008, 153–8
    Singer and Lamm, op. cit.

5. *For the 2004 empathy study of couples receiving painful electric shocks to their hands, see* T. Singer, B. Seymour, J. O'Doherty, *et al.*, 'Empathy for pain involves the affective but not sensory components of pain', *Science* 303, 2004, 1,157–61

6. *For the 2006 study showing that the degree of brain activation is proportional to our reading of the pain, see* A. Avenanti, I. M. Paluelo, I. Bufalari, *et al.*, 'Stimulus-driven modulation of motor-evoked potentials during observation of others' pain', *Neuroimage* 32, 2006, 316–24

7. *For evidence that we detect pain intensity in others through mirror neurons and 'empathy neurons', see* M. V. Saarela, Y. Hlushchuk, A. C. de C. Williams, M. Schürmann, E. Kalso and R. Hari, 'The compassionate brain: humans detect intensity of pain from another's face', *Cerebral Cortex* 17(1), 2007, 230–7

8. *For the 2007 study showing activation of specific brain regions during pain in a specific part of the body, see* I. Bufalari, T. Aprile, A. Avenanti, F. Di Russo, *et al.*, 'Empathy for pain and touch in the human somatosensory cortex', *Cerebral Cortex* 17, 2007,

2,553–61; *also* Y. Cheng, C–P. Lin, C–Y. Yang, *et al.*, 'The perception of pain in others modulates somatosensory oscillations', *Neuroimage* 40, 2008, 1,833–40

9. *For the physical-emotional effects of seeing someone suffer, see* S. D. Preston and F. B. M. de Waal, 'Empathy: its ultimate and proximate bases', *Behavioral and Brain Sciences* 25, 2002, 1–72

10. Diane Berke, *The Gentle Smile: Practicing Oneness in Daily Life*, Crossroad Publishing Company, New York, 1995

11. *For the 2008 study of expert and novice meditators doing compassion meditations, see* A. Lutz, J. Brefczynski-Lewis, T. Johnstone and R. J. Davidson, 'Regulation of the neural circuitry of emotion by compassion meditation: effects of meditative expertise', *PLoS ONE*, 3(3), 2008, e1897

12. *For the 2009 study linking compassion with the immune system, see* T. W. W. Pace, L. T. Negi, D. D. Adame, S. P. Cole, T. I. Sivillia, T. D. Brown, M. J. Issa and C. L. Raison, 'Effect of compassion meditation on neuroendocrine, innate immune and behavioural responses to psychosocial stress', *Psychoneuroendocrinology* 34, 2009, 87–98

CHAPTER 3: HAVING THE NERVE TO BE COMPASSIONATE

1. *For the 2009 study linking compassion, vagal tone and similarity to strong or vulnerable groups, see* C. Oveis, E. J. Horberg and D. Keltner, 'Compassion, pride, and social intuitions of self-other similarity', *Journal of Personality and Social Psychology* (in press at time of writing)

2. *For research on power and compassion, see* G. A. van Cleef, C. Oveis, I. van der Lowe, A. LuoKogan, J. Goetz and D. Keltner, 'Power, distress, and compassion', *Psychological Science* 19(12), 2008, 1,315–22

3. *For the study where sad faces activated the amygdala, see* P. J. Whalen, *et al.*, 'Masked presentations of emotional facial expressions modulate amygdala activity without explicit knowledge', *Journal of Neuroscience* 18, 1998, 411–18

4. *For the study of watching people playing an economics game with the sound muted, see* Dacher Keltner, *Born to Be Good: The Science of a Meaningful Life*, Norton, New York, 2009

5. *For the studies showing the children with highest vagal tone are most helpful in class, see:*
    N. Eisenberg, R. A. Fabes, B. Murphy, P. Maszk, M. Smith and M. Karbon, 'The role of emotionality and regulation in children's social functioning: a longitudinal study', *Child Development* 66(5), 1995, 1,360–84
    —, 'The relations of children's dispositional empathy-related responding to their emotionality, regulation, and social functioning', *Developmental Psychology* 32, 1996, 195–209

6. *For the study where children watched videotapes of other children injured in accidents, see* N. Eisenberg, R. A. Fabes, P. A. Miller, J. Fultz, R. Shell, R. M. Mathy and R. R. Reno, 'Relation of sympathy and personal distress to prosocial behaviour: a multi-method study', *Journal of Personality and Social Psychology* 57(1), 1989, 55–66, *and* N. Eisenberg, M. Schaller, R. A Fabes, D. Bustamante, R. M. Mathy, R. Shell, and K. Rhodes, 'Differentiation of personal distress and sympathy in children and adults', *Developmental Psychology* 24, 1988, 766–75

7. *For the 2005 study where bereaved people wrote about their past, see* M. F. O'Connor, J. J. B. Allen and A. W. Waszniak, 'Emotional disclosure for whom? A study of vagal tone in bereavement', *Biological Psychology* 68, 2005, 135–46

8. *For a description of the study where university students with high vagal tone handled stress better, see* Keltner, op. cit.

9. *For the Kevin Tracey inflammatory reflex paper, see* K. J. Tracey, 'The inflammatory reflex', *Nature* 420, 2002, 853–9; *also* H. Wang, *et al.*, 'Nicotinic acetylcholine receptor alpha7 subunit is an essential regulator of inflammation', *Nature* 421, 2003, 384–8

10. *For the study where stimulating the vagus nerve can prevent multiple organ damage, see* J. M. Huston, *et al.*, 'Transcutaneous vagus nerve stimulation reduces serum high mobility group box 1 levels and improves survival in murine sepsis', *Critical Care Medicine* 35(12), 2007, 2, 762–8

11. Quoted in K. McGowan, 'Can we cure aging?', 4 December 2007,
    http://discovermagazine.com/2007/dec/can-we-cure-aging

12. *For studies on telomere shortening and ageing and a link with inflammation, see:*
    A. Aviv, 'Telomeres and human aging: facts and fibs', *Science of Aging Knowledge Environment* 51, 2004, pe43
    —, 'The epidemiology of human telomeres', *Journal of Gerontology Series A: Biological Sciences and Medical Sciences* 63(9), 2008, 979–83
    T. DeMeyer, E. R. Rietzschel, M. L. DeBuyzere, W. Van Criekinge and S. Bekaert, 'Studying telomeres in a longitudinal population based study', *Frontiers in Bioscience* 13, 2008, 2,960–70

13. *For the 2009 study where vagus nerve stimulation increased nitric oxide levels, see* K. E. Brack, V. H. Patel, R. Mantravardi, J. H. Coote and G. A. Ng, 'Direct evidence of nitric oxide release from neuronal nitric oxide synthase activation in the left ventrical as a result of cervical vagus nerve stimulation', *Journal of Physiology* 587(12), 2009, 3,045–54; *also* V. Patel, K. E. Brack, J. H. Coote and G. A. Ng, 'Vagus nerve stimulation releases nitric oxide in the cardiac ventricle: evidence from fluorescence

studies in the innervated isolated heart', *Circulation* 114(II), 2006, 270, Abstract 1413

14. *For increasing nitric oxide levels by breathing deeply through the nose, see* http://health.discovery.com/fansites/dr-oz/aging/tips.html (accessed 24 September 2009)

15. *For examples of studies showing that meditation and hypnosis can reduce inflammation, see* P. D. Shenefelt, 'Relaxation, Meditation, and Hypnosis for Skin Disorders and Procedures' in B. N. DeLuca (ed.), *Mind-Body and Relaxation Research Focus*, Nova Science Publishers, Inc., Hauppage, 2008, pp.45–63

16. *For the suggestion that prayer and acupuncture might affect the vagus nerve, see* C. Libert, 'Inflammation: a nervous connection', *Nature* 421, 2003, 328–9

17. *For the 2002 study where endotoxin-induced fever and interleukin-II levels in rats were reduced by acupuncture, see* Y. S. Son, H-J. Park, O-B. Kwon, S-C. Jung, H-C. Shin and S. Lim, 'Antipyretic effects of acupuncture on the lipopolysaccharide-induced fever and expression of interleukin-6 and interleukin-1β mRNAs in the hypothalamus of rats', *Neuroscience Letters* 319, 2002, 45–8

18. *For the study linking religious service attendance and reduced levels of pro-inflammatory cytokines in diabetic patients, see* D. E. King, A. G. Mainous III and W. Pearson, 'C-reactive protein, diabetes, and attendance at religious services', *International Journal of Psychiatry Medicine* 25(7), 2002, 1,172–6

19. *For the 2001 study linking religious service attendance and reduced levels of pro-inflammatory cytokines, see* D. E. King, A. G. Mainous III, T. E. Steyer and W. Pearson, 'The relationship between attendance at religious service and cardiovascular inflammatory markers', *International Journal of Psychiatry Medicine* 31(4), 2001, 415–25

CHAPTER 4: HOW KINDNESS CHANGES THE BRAIN

1. *For an excellent and accessible book about neuroplasticity, see* Norman Doidge, MD, *The Brain That Changes Itself*, Viking Penguin, New York, 2007

2. *For the neuroplasticity through juggling study, see:*
   B. Draganski, C. Gaser, V. Busch, G. Schuierer, U. Bogdahn and A. May, 'Changes in gray matter induced by training', *Nature* 427(6,972), 2004, 311–12
   J. Driemeyer, J. Boyke, C. Gaser, C. Büchel and A. May, 'Changes in gray matter induced by learning … revisited', *PLoS ONE* 3(7), 2008, e2669

3. *For the study where 170 genes were affected by stress, see* S. Roy, S. Khanna, P. E. Yeh, C. Rink, W. B. Malarkey, J. K. Kiecolt-Glaser, B. Laskowski, R. Glaser and C. K. Sen, 'Wound site neurophil in response to psychological stress in young men', *Gene Expression* 12(4–6), 2005, 273–87

4. *For the 2008 study where the relaxation response impacted 1,561 genes, see* J. A Dusek, H. H. Otu, A. L. Wohlhueter, M. Bhasin, L. F. Zerbini, M. G. Joseph, H. Benson and T. A. Liberman, 'Genomic counter-stress changes induced by the relaxation response', *PLoS ONE* 3(7), 2008, e2567, 1–8

CHAPTER 5: OXYTOCIN IN THE BRAIN

1. *For a reference to the study where people receiving oxytocin looked in people's eyes in photos for longer, see* 'Can Oxytocin Ease Shyness?', *Time*, July 21, 2008. M. J. Stephey wrote, 'Without oxytocin people would be far less inclined to seek social interaction, let alone fall in love and mate for life.'

2. *For the Trust Game study where participants were betrayed, see* T. Baumgartner, M. Heinrichs, A. Vonlanthen, U. Fischbacher and E. Fehr, 'Oxytocin shapes the neural circuitry of trust and trust adaptation in humans', *Neuron* 58, 2008, 639–50

3.   *For the study linking trust with a nation's fortunes, see* S. Knack
     and P. J. Zak, 'Building Trust: Public Policy, Interpersonal Trust,
     and Economic Development', obtained from http://goldmark.
     org/livia/misc/zak-trust.pdf (accessed on 25 September 2009);
     also P. J. Zak and S. Knack, 'Trust and growth', *The Economic
     Journal* 11, 2001, 295–321

4.   *For the statistics on dropping levels of trust, see* Richard Layard,
     Happiness: Lessons from a New Science, Penguin, New York,
     2005

5.   *For the study of oxytocin and looking at faces conditioned to
     produce fear, see* P. Petrovic, R. Kalisch, T. Singer and R. Dolan,
     'Oxytocin attenuates affective evaluations of conditioned faces
     and amygdala activity', *Journal of Neuroscience* 28(26), 2008,
     6,607–15; *also* G. Domes, *et al.*, 'Oxytocin attenuates amygdala
     responses to emotional faces regardless of valence', *Biological
     Psychiatry* 62, 2007, 1, 187–90

6.   *For the study where men who took oxytocin were better at
     remembering faces, see* U. Rimmele, K. Hediger, M. Heinrichs
     and P. Klaver, 'Oxytocin makes a face in memory familiar',
     Journal of Neuroscience 29(1), 2009, 38–42

7.   *For reference to the study where men and women found
     strangers more attractive when they had received oxytocin, see*
     E. Callaway, 'Love hormone boosts strangers' sex appeal', *New
     Scientist*, 9 April 2009

8.   *For the study where oxytocin improved 20 men's ability to read
     emotions, see* G. Domes, M. Heinrichs, A. Michel, C. Berger and
     S. C. Herpetz, 'Oxytocin improves "mind reading" in humans',
     Biological Psychiatry 61, 2007, 731–3

9.   *For the studies linking oxytocin with the improved ability in autistic
     adults to read emotions in voices as well as read and interpret
     facial expressions, see* E. Hollander, S. Novotny, M. Hanratty,

R. Yaffe, C. M. DeCaria, B. R. Aronowitz and S. Mosovich, 'Oxytocin infusion reduces repetitive behaviours in adults with autistic and Asperger's disorders', *Neuropsychopharmacology* 28, 2003, 193–8

10. *For the studies linking oxytocin with improved ability to read and interpret facial expressions in autistic adults, see* ibid.

11. *For the 2007 study where oxytocin improved generosity by 80 per cent, see* P. J. Zak, A. A. Stanton and S. Ahmadi, 'Oxytocin increases generosity in humans', *PLoS ONE* 11, 2007, e1128

CHAPTER 6: WAYS TO PRODUCE OXYTOCIN

1. *For the inspirational effects of elevation in producing oxytocin, see* J. A. Silvers and J. Haidt, 'Moral elevation can induce nursing', *Emotion* 8(2), 2008, 291–5

2. *For the effects of expressing emotions, see* M. Tops, J. M. Van Peer and J. Korf, 'Individual differences in emotional expressivity predict oxytocin responses to cortisol administration: relevance to breast cancer?', *Biological Psychology* 75(2), 2007, 119–23

3. *For the ability of massage to produce oxytocin, see* V. B. Morhenn, J. W. Park, E. Piper and P. J. Zak, 'Monetary sacrifice among strangers is mediated by endogenous oxytocin release after physical contact', *Evolution and Human Behaviour* 29, 2008, 375–83

4. *For the 38-couple study linking partner support with increased oxytocin, see* K. M. Grewen, S. S. Girdler, J. Amico and K. C. Light, 'Effects of partner support on resting oxytocin, cortisol, norepinephrine, and blood pressure before and after warm partner contact', *Psychosomatic Medicine* 67, 2005, 531–8

5. *For a study showing that anticipation of contact might increase oxytocin levels, see* R. White-Traut, K. Watanabe, H.

Pournajafi-Nazarloo, D. Schwertz, A. Bell and C. S. Carter, 'Detection of salivary oxytocin levels in lactating women', *Developmental Psychobiology* 51(4), 2009, 367–73

6. *For the 34-couple study, see* Holt-Lunstad, *et al.*, 'Influence of a "warm touch" support enhancement intervention among married couples on ambulatory blood pressure, oxytocin, alpha amylase, and cortisol', *Psychosomatic Medicine* 70, 2008, 976–85

7. *For the study linking more hugs with more oxytocin, see* K. C. Light, K. M. Grewen and J. A. Amico, 'More frequent partner hugs and higher oxytocin levels are linked to lower blood pressure and heart rate in premenopausal women', *Biological Psychology* 69, 2005, 5–21

8. *For a reference to the study linking long-term survival of heart patients with having a pet, see* Dr Mimi Guarneri, *The Heart Speaks*, Simon & Schuster, 2006

9. *For a description of the study of the 55 dog owners in Japan, see* E. Callaway, 'Pet dogs rival humans for emotional satisfaction', *New Scientist*, 14 January 2009

10. *For the Harvard study linking caring for a plant with longer life, see* E. J. Langer and J. Rodin, 'The effects of choice and enhanced personal responsibility for the aged: a field experiment in an institutional setting', *Journal of Personality and Social Psychology* 34(2), 1976, 191–8

CHAPTER 7: OXYTOCIN, DIGESTION AND INFLAMMATION

1. *For the 2004 study where oxytocin and oxytocin receptors were found in gut biopsies, see* H-J. Monstein, N. Grahn, M. Truedsson and B. Ohisson, 'Oxytocin and oxytocin-receptor rRNA expression in the human gastrointestinal tract: a polymerase chain reaction study', *Regulatory Peptides* 119(1–2), 2004, 39–44

2. *For review of the promoting effects of oxytocin on gastric motility, see* B. Ohlsson and S. Janciauskiene, 'New insights into the understanding of gastrointestinal dysmotility', *Drug Targets Insights* 2, 2007, 229–37

3. *For the study where oxytocin is released into the bloodstream on eating and helps mixing and grinding, see* B. Ohlsson, M. L. Forsling, J. F. Rehfield, *et al.*, 'Cholecystokinin leads to increased oxytocin secretion in healthy women', *European Journal of Surgery* 168, 2002, 114–18

4. *For the first study showing oxytocin's role in gastric emptying, see* M. Hashmonai, S. Torem, S. Argov, *et al.*, 'Prolonged post-vagotomy gastric atony treated with oxytocin', *British Journal of Surgery* 66, 1979, 550–51

5. *For the proof of the pudding, so to speak, see* B. Ohlsson, O. Björgell, O. Eckberg, *et al.*, 'The oxytocin/vasopressin receptor antagonist atosiban delays the gastric emptying of a semisolid meal compared to saline in humans', *BMC Gastroenterology* 6, 2006, 11

6. *For the study showing that children with recurring stomach pain can have low blood levels of oxytocin, see* G. Alfven, 'Plasma oxytocin in children with recurrent abdominal pain', *Journal of Pediatrics, Gastroenterology and Nutrition* 38, 2004, 513–17

7. *For the study linking oxytocin deficiency in diabetic patients with gastric dysmotility, see* J. Borg, O. Melander, L. Johansson, K. Uvnäs-Moberg and B. Ohlsson, 'Gastroparesis is associated with oxytocin deficiency, oesophageal dysmotility with hyper-CCKemia, and autonomic neuropathy with hypergastrinema', *BMC Gastroenterology* 25, 2009, 9–17

8. *For the study showing that oxytocin helps move matter through the colon, see* B. Ohlsson, G. Ringström, H. Abrahamsson, *et al.*, 'Oxytocin stimulates colonic motor activity in healthy women', *Neurogastroenterology and Motility* 16, 2004, 233–40

9. For a study that found IBS patients to have low levels of oxytocin, see K. Uvnäs-Moberg, I. Arn, I. Theorell, et al., 'Gastrin, somatostatin and oxytocin levels in patients with functional disorders of the gastrointestinal tract and their response to feeding and interaction', Journal of Psychosomatic Research 35, 1991, 525–33

10. For the connection between low levels of oxytocin, fibromyalgia, depression and IBS, see A. Frasch, T. Zetzche, A. Steiger, et al., 'Reduction of plasma oxytocin levels in patients suffering from major depression', Advances in Experimental Medicine and Biology 395, 1995, 257–8; also U. M. Anderberg and K. Uvnäs-Moberg, 'Plasma oxytocin levels in female fibromyalgia syndrome patients', Z. Rheumatology 59, 2000, 373–9

11. For the study where IBS pain was reduced on receiving oxytocin, see D. Louvel, M. Delvaux, A. Felez, et al., 'Oxytocin increases thresholds of colonic visceral perception in patients with irritable bowel syndrome', Gut 39, 1996, 741–7

12. For the study showing that oxytocin reduces inflammation caused by bacterial infection, see M. Clodi, G. Vila, R. Geyeregger, M. Riedl, T. M. Stulnig, J. Struck, T. A. Luger and A. Luger, 'Oxytocin alleviates the neuroendocrine and cytokine response to bacterial endotoxin in healthy men', American Journal of Physiology, Endocrinology and Metabolism 295, 2008, E686–91

13. For the early studies showing that oxytocin increases vagus nerve activation, see:
M. Raggenbass, M. Dubois-Dauphin, S. Charpak and J. J. Dreifuss, 'Neurons in the dorsal motor nucleus of the vagus nerve are excited by oxytocin in the rat but not in the guinea pig', Proceedings of the National Academy of Sciences USA 84 (11), 1987, 3,926–30
M. J. McCann and R. C. Rogers, 'Oxytocin excites gastric-related neurons in rat dorsal vagal complex', Journal of Physiology 428, 1990, 95–108

14. *For the study where oxytocin suppressed the growth of non-small cell lung cancer, see* S. Zhong, C. R. Fields, N. Su, Y. X. Pan and K. D. Robertson, 'Pharmacologic inhibition of epigenetic modifications, coupled with gene expression profiling, reveals novel targets of aberrant DNA methylation and histone deacetylation in lung cancer', *Oncogene* 26, 2007, 2,621–34

15. *For the effect of oxytocin on some other cancers, see* P. Cassoni, A. Sapino, T. Parroco, B. Chini and G. Bussolanti, 'Oxytocin and oxytocin receptors in cancer cells and proliferation', *Journal of Neuroendocrinology* 16, 2004, 362–4

16. *For the study linking emotional expression and breast cancer with oxytocin, see* J. M. Van Peer and J. Korf, 'Individual differences in emotional expressivity predict oxytocin responses to cortisol administration: relevance to breast cancer', *Biological Psychiatry* 75(2), 2007, 119–23

17. *For the varying effects of oxytocin on the prostate, depending on hormone levels, see* K. Whittington, B. Connors, K. King, S. Assinder, K. Hogarth, H. Nicholson, M. Xiong and G. Elson, 'The effect of oxytocin on cell proliferation in the human prostate is modulated by gonadal steroids: implications for benign hyperplasia and carcinoma of the prostate', *Prostate* 67, 2007, 1,132–42

***CHAPTER 8: * OXYTOCIN AND THE HEART**

1. *For the 1996 study finding that oxytocin bound to its receptor in the human aorta, see* H. Yazawa, A. Hirasawa, K. Horie, Y. Saita, E. Lida, K. Honda and G. Tsujimoto, 'Oxytocin receptors expressed and coupled to Ca2+ signalling in a human vascular smooth muscle cell line', *British Journal of Pharmacology* 117, 1996, 799–804

2. *For the 1999 study finding that oxytocin bound to its receptor in the right atrium, see* N. J. Cicutti, C. E. Smyth, O. P. Rosaeg

and M. Wilkinson, 'Oxytocin receptor binding in rat and human heart', *Canadian Journal of Cardiology* 15(11), 1999, 1,267–73

3. *For the 1999 study where oxytocin was shown to bind to its receptors in the aorta, pulmonary artery and human umbilical vein cells, see* M. Thibonnier, *et al.*, 'Human vascular endothelial cells express oxytocin receptors', *Endocrinology* 140(3), 1999, 1,301–9

4. *For links between oxytocin and nitric oxide release, see:*
   L. Haraldsen, V. Söderström and G. Nilsson, 'Oxytocin stimulates cerebral blood flow in rainbow trout (*Oncorhynchus mykiss*) through a nitric oxide dependent mechanism', *Brain Research* 929(1), 2002, 10–14
   H. Oyama, Y. Suzuki, S. Satoh, Y. Kajita, M. Shibuya and K. Sugita, 'Role of nitric oxide in the cerebral vasodilatory responses to vasopressin and oxytocin in dogs', *Journal of Cerebral Blood Flow and Metabolism* 13(2), 1993, 285–90

5. *For a study showing that oxytocin stimulates the release of ANP, see* J. Gutkowska, M. Jankowski, C. Lambert, S. Mukaddam-Daher, H. H. Zingg and S. M. McCann, 'Oxytocin releases atrial natriuretic peptide by combining with oxytocin receptors in the heart', *Proceedings of the National Academy of Sciences USA* 94, 1997, 11,704–9

6. *For the 2008 study where oxytocin was shown to protect against atherosclerosis, see* A. Szeto, D. A. Nation, A. J. Mendez, J. Dominguez-Bendela, L. G. Brooks, N. Schneiderman and P. M. McCabe, 'Oxytocin attenuates NADP-dependent superoxide activity and IL-6 secretion in macrophages and vascular cells', *American Journal of Endrocrinology and Metabolism* 295, 2008, E1,495–501

Note: In this research, the scientists studied the mechanism of how atherosclerosis develops and found that oxytocin could slow the process. I conclude, therefore, that oxytocin protects against atherosclerosis although no actual human study has yet been attempted to show this.

7. *For the 150-couple study linking hostility to atherosclerosis, see:* T. W. Smith, C. Berg, B. N. Uchino, P. Florsheim and G. Pearce, 'Marital conflict behaviour and coronary artery calcification', Paper presented at the American Psychosomatic Society's 64th Annual Meeting, Denver, CO, 3 March 2006
    J. K. Kiecolt-Glaser, T. J. Loving, J, R. Stowell, W. B. Malarkey, S. Lemeshow, S. L. Dickinson and R. Glaser, 'Hostile marital interactions, proinflammatory cytokine production, and wound healing', *Archives of General Psychiatry* 62, 2005, 1,377–84

8. *For the study where rabbits were protected against atherosclerosis through being petted, see* R. M. Nerem, M. J. Levesque and J. F. Cornhill, 'Social environment as a factor in diet-induced atherosclerosis', *Science* 208, 1980, 1,475–6

9. *For the study where oxytocin stimulated angiogenesis, see* M. G. Cattaneo, G. Lucci and L. M. Vicentini, 'Oxytocin stimulates in vitro angiogenesis via a Pyk-2/Src-dependent mechanism', *Experimental Cell Research* 315(18), 2009, 3,210–19

10. *For the study showing that wounds healed at only 60 per cent of the normal rate on account of a marital conflict, see* J. K. Kiecolt-Glaser, T. J. Loving, J. R. Stockwell, W. B. Malarkey, S. Lemeshow, S. L. Dickinson and R. Glaser, 'Hostile marital interactions, proinflammatory cytokine production, and wound healing', *Archive of General Psychiatry* 62(12), 2005, 1,377–84; *also* E. Broadbent, K. J. Petrie, P. G. Alley and R. J. Booth, 'Psychological stress impairs early wound repair following surgery', *Psychosomatic Medicine* 65(5), 2003, 865–9; *and* L. M. Christian, J. E. Graham, D. A. Padgett, R. Glaser and J. K. Kiecolt-Glaser, 'Stress and wound healing', *Neuroimmunomodulation* 13(5–6), 2006, 337–46

11. *For the 2004 study of the effect of oxytocin on skin wounds,*

see C. E. Detillion, T. K. Craft, E. R. Glasper, B. J. Prendergast and A. C. DeVries, 'Social facilitation of wound healing', *Psychoneuroendocrinology* 29(8), 2004, 1,004–11

12. *For the 2009 study of the effect of oxytocin on burn wounds, see* A. Vitalo, J. Fricchione, M. Casali, Y. Berdichevsky, E. A. Hoge, A. L. Rauch, F. Berthiaume, M. L. Yarmush, H. Benson, G. L. Fricchione and J. B. Levine, 'Nest making and oxytocin comparably promote wound healing in isolated reared rats', *PLoS ONE* 4(5), 2009, e5523

13. *For the 2004 report that 90 per cent of heart patients who exercised were free of heart problems within a year, visit:* http://www.msnbc.msn.com/id/32618616/ns/health-heart_health/

14. *For the 2007 study of heart patients producing new stem cells by riding a bike, see* 'Exercise can help a bad heart repair itself' at: http://www.msnbc.msn.com/id/20606123/ (2007)

15. *For the 2009 study that used carbon-14 to show the replenishment of heart muscle cells, see* O. Bergmann, R. D. Bhardwaj, S. Bernard, S. Zdunek, F. Heider-Barnabé, S. Walsh, J. Zupicich, K. Alkass, B. A. Buchholz, H. Druid, S. Jovinge and J. Frisen, 'Evidence for cardiomyocyte renewal in humans', *Science* 324(5923), 2009, 98–102

16. *For the study showing that injecting NRG1 initiated the cell division of heart muscle cells, see* K. Bersell, S. Arab, B. Haring and B. Kühn, 'Neuregulin1/ErbB4 signaling induces cardiomyocyte proliferation and repair of heart injury', *Cell* 138(2), 2009, 257–70

17. *For the 2008 study that showed the role of oxytocin in the conversion of stem cells into heart cells in a foetus, see* N. Gassanov, D. Devost, B. Danalache, N. Noiseux, M. Jankowski, H. H. Zingg and J. Gutkowska, 'Functional activity of the carboxyl-terminally extended oxytocin precursor peptide during cardiac

differentiation of embryonic stem cells', *Stem Cells* 26, 2008, 45–54

18. *For a study that links low birth weight with abuse during pregnancy, see* M. S. Yang, S. Y. Ho, F. H. Chou, S. J. Chang and Y. C. Ko, 'Physical abuse during pregnancy and risk of low-birthweight infants among aborigines in Taiwan', *Public Health* 120(6), 2006, 557–62

CHAPTER 9: SUPPORTING THE HEART

1. *For information on the Roseto study, visit:* http://www.uic.edu/classes/osci/osci590/14_2%20The%20Roseto%20Effect.htm (accessed 13 October 2009)

2. *The study of the men of Japanese ancestry living in Hawaii can be found in* Dr Mimi Guarneri, *The Heart Speaks*, Simon & Schuster, 2006

3. *The 2008 report of heart disease statistics was obtained from:* http://www.heartstats.org (accessed 21 September 2009)

4. *For the study of the angina patients who had love and support, which equated to less coronary artery disease, see* Martin Seligman, *Learned Optimism: How to Change your Mind and your Life*, New York Free Press, New York, 1998

5. Guarneri, op. cit.

6. *For the 1992 study linking living alone with the increased risk of a heart attack, see* R. B. Case, A. J. Moss, N. Case, M. McDermott and S. Eberly, 'Living alone after myocardial infarction: impact on prognosis', *Journal of the American Medical Association* 267(4), 1992, 515–19

7. *For the study linking small social networks with increased risk of atherosclerosis, see* W. J. Kop, D. S. Berman, H. Gransar, N. D. Wong, R. Miranda-Peats, M. D. White, M. Shin, M. Bruce, D. S. Krantz and A. Rozanski, 'Social network and coronary

artery calcification in asymptomatic individuals', *Psychosomatic Medicine* 67, 2005, 343–52

8. *For the 1979 study linking number of social ties with mortality rate, see* L. F. Berkman and S. L. Syme, 'Social networks, host resistance, and mortality: a nine-year follow-up study of Alamede County residents', *American Journal of Epidemiology* 109(2), 1979, 186–204

9. *For the 1987 study of 17,000 Swedish people, see* T. E. Seeman, G. A. Kaplan, L. Knudsen, R. Cohen and J. Guralink, 'Social ties and mortality in the elderly: a comparative analysis of age-dependent patterns of association', *American Journal of Epidemiology* 126, 1987, 714–23

10. *For the 30-year wives and mothers study showing that multiple roles are associated with a longer lifespan, see* P. Moen, D. Dempster-McClain and R. M. Williams, 'Social intergration and longevity: an event history of women's roles and resilience', *American Sociological Review* 54, 1989, 635–47

11. *For the evidence of social support protecting against arthritis and TB, see* J. Tomaka, S. Thompson and R. Palacios, 'The relation of social isolation, loneliness, and social support to disease outcomes among the elderly', *Journal of Aging and Health* 18(3), 2006, 359–84

12. *For the National Longitudinal Mortality Study, see* N. J. Johnson, E. Backlund, P. D. Sorlie and C. A Loveless, 'Marital status and mortality: the national longitudinal mortality study', *Annals of Epidemiology* 10(4), 2000, 224–38

13. *For the British Regional Heart Study, see* S. Ibrahim, G. Wannamethee, A. McCallum, M. Walker and A. G. Shaper, 'Marital status, change in marital status and mortality in middle-aged British men', *American Journal of Epidemiology* 142(8), 1995, 834–42

14. *For evidence that it's not the marriage itself but the quality of relationship that matters most, see* V. Chandra, M. Szklo, R. Goldber and J. Tonascia, 'The impact of marital status on survival after an acute myocardial infarction: a population study', *Journal of Epidemiology* 117, 1983, 320–25

15. *For the 1986 study that found that an unhappy marriage was linked with a 25-fold increase in depression, see* M. M. Weissman, 'Advances in psychiatric epidemiology: rates and risks for major depression', *American Journal of Public Health* 77, 1987, 445–51

16. *For the 1994 study linking unhappy marriages with a 10 times greater risk of depression, see* K. D. O'Leary, J. L. Christian and N. R. Mendell, 'A closer look at the link between marital discord and depressive symptomatology', *Journal of Social and Clinical Psychology* 13, 1994, 33–41

17. *For the 2000 study of women heart patients that linked marital stress with a 2.9-fold increase in risk of a further coronary event, see* K. Orth-Gomer, S. Wamala, M. Horsten, K. Schenck-Gustafsson, N. Schneiderman and M. Mittleman, 'Marital stress worsens prognosis in women with coronary heart disease: the Stockholm female coronary risk study', *Journal of the American Medical Association* 284, 2000, 3,008–14

18. *For the 2001 study of congestive heart failure patients linking marital quality with likelihood of survival, see* J. Coyne, M. Rohrbaugh, V. Shoham, J. Sonnega, J. Nicklas and J. Cranford, 'Prognostic importance of marital quality for survival after congestive heart failure', *American Journal of Cardiology* 88, 2001, 526–9

19. *For the 2006 four-year follow-up, see* M. Rohrbaugh, V. Shoham and J. Coyne, 'Effect of marital quality on eight-year survival of patients with heart failure', *American Journal of Cardiology* 98(8), 2006, 1,069–72

20. *For the 2004 study showing that stable partnerships slow the rate of progression of HIV to AIDS, see* J. Young, S. De Geest, R. Spirig, M. Flepp, M. Rickenbach, H. Furrer, E. Bernasconi, B. Hirschel, A. Telenti, P. Vernazza, M. Battegay and H. C. Bucher, 'Stable partnership and progression to AIDS or death in HIV infected patients receiving highly active antiretroviral therapy: Swiss HIV cohort study', *British Medical Journal* 328, 2004, 15

21. *For the study linking marital dissatisfaction with metabolic syndrome, see* W. M. Troxel, K. A. Matthews, L. C. Gallo and L. H. Kuller, 'Marital quality and occurrence of the metabolic syndrome in women', *Archives of Internal Medicine* 165, 2005, 1,022–7

22. *For the 2008 study of heart failure patients that showed that the use of the word, 'we' was associated with improved symptoms, see* M. J. Rohnbaugh, M. R. Mehl, V. Shoham, E. S. Reilly and G. A. Ewy, 'Prognostic significance of spouse we talk in couples coping with heart failure', *Journal of Consultation and Clinical Psychology* 76(5), 2008, 781–9

23. *For studies linking hostility with a host of conditions and biomarkers of disease, see:*
    C. K. Ewart, C. B. Taylor, H. C. Kraemer and W. S. Agras, 'High blood pressure and marital discord: not being nasty matters more than being nice', *Health Psychology* 10, 1991, 155–63
    J. K. Kiecolt-Glaser, W. B. Malarkey, M. Chee, T. Newton, J. T. Cacioppo, H. Y. Mao and R. Glaser, 'Negative behaviour during marital conflict is associated with immunological down-regulation', *Psychosomatic Medicine* 55, 1993, 395–409
    W. Malarkey, J. K. Kiecolt-Glaser, D. Pearl and R. Glaser, 'Hostile behaviour during marital conflict alters pituitary and adrenal hormones', *Psychosomatic Medicine* 56, 1994, 41–51
    J. K. Kiecolt-Glaser, R. Glaser, J. T. Cacioppo, R. C. MacCallum, M. Snydersmith, C. Kim and W. B. Malarkey, 'Marital conflict in older adults: endocrinological and immunological correlates', *Psychosomatic Medicine* 59, 1997, 339–49

24. *For the 2006 study linking hostility and cynicism with increased interleukin-6 levels, see* E. Sjogren, P. Leanderson, M. Kristenson and J. Ernerudh, 'Interleukin-6 levels in relation to psychosocial factors: studies or serum, saliva, and in vitro production by blood mononuclear cells', *Brain Behaviour and Immunity* 20, 2006, 270–78

25. *For the 2006 study showing that improved communication can reduce stress hormone levels, see* T. F. Robles, V. A. Shaffer, W. B. Malarkey and J. K. Kiecolt-Glaser, 'Positive behaviours during marital conflict: influences on stress hormones', *Journal of Social and Personal Relationships* 23(2), 2006, 305–25

26. *For the study on the heart benefits of doing another's dirty laundry, see* Robert A. Emmons, *Thanks: How the New Science of Gratitude Can Make You Happier*, Houghton Mifflin Harcourt, 2007

27. *For a 2008 study showing the cortisol-lowering effects of intimacy, see* B. Ditzen, C. Hoppmann and P. Klumb, 'Positive couple interactions and daily cortisol: on the stress-protecting role of intimacy', *Psychosomatic Medicine* 70, 2008, 883–9

28. *For the 1994 study that found that emotional social support was linked with lower stress hormone levels, see* T. Seeman, L. Berkman, D. Blazer and J. Rowe, 'Social ties and support and neuroendocrine function: the MacArthur studies of successful ageing', *Annals of Behavioural Medicine* 16, 1994, 95–106

29. *For a study that showed that social ties need some form of intimacy to be health-giving, see* L. Berkman, 'The role of social relations in health promotion', *Psychosomatic Medicine* 57, 1995, 245–54

30. *For a study linking lack of intimate contact with increased sympathetic nervous system response, see* S. Knox, T. Theorell, J. Svensson and D. Waller, 'The relation of social support and working environment to medical variables associated with

elevated blood pressure in young males: a structural model', *Social Science and Medicine* 21, 1985, 523–31

31. *For 1998 studies showing the protective effects of social support on the heart, see* S. Knox and K. Uvnas-Moberg, 'Social isolation and cardiovascular disease: an atherosclerotic pathway?', *Psychoneuroendocrinology* 23, 1998, 877–90; *and* K. Uvnas-Moberg, 'Oxytocin may mediate the benefits of positive social interaction and emotions', *Psychoneuroendocrinology* 23, 1998, 819–35

CHAPTER 10: WHY BABIES NEED LOVE

1. *For an excellent book containing copious amounts of information relating an infant's early emotional environment, the growth of its brain and its overall health growing up, see* Sue Gerhardt, *Why Love Matters: How Affection Shapes a Baby's Brain*, Routledge, East Sussex, 2004

2. *For information on the growth of the infant's brain and its emotional development, see* Allan N. Schore, *Affect Regulation and the Origin of the Self: The Neurobiology of Emotional Development*, Lawrence Erlbaum Associates, Inc., New Jersey, 1994

3. *For the study showing how the left and right frontal regions of an infant's brain are activated by happy or sad behaviour respectively, see* R. Davidson and N. Fox, 'Asymmetrical brain activity discriminates between positive v. negative affective stimuli in human infants', *Science* 218, 1992, 1,235–7

4. *For the Wayne State University study of Romanian orphans with reduced activity in several brain regions, see* H. Chugani, *et al.*, 'Local brain functional activity following early deprivation: a study of post-institutionalised Romanian orphans', *Neuroimage* 14, 2001, 1,290–301

5. *For information on the Bucharest Early Intervention Project, visit:* http://www.crin.org/docs/PPT%20BEIP%20Group.pdf (accessed 13 October 2009)

6. *For the 2009 Harvard study of the impact of institutionalized care on memory and executive function, see* K. J. Bos, N. Fox, C. H. Zeanah and C. A. Nelson III, 'Effects of early psychosocial deprivation on the development of memory and executive function', *Frontier Behavioural Neuroscience* 3, 2009, 16

7. *For the 2009 St. John Fisher College study showing the benefits of fostering, see* M. M. Ghera, P. J. Marshall, N. A. Fox, C. H. Zeanah, C. A. Nelson, A. T. Smyke and D. Guthrie, 'The effects of foster care intervention on socially deprived institutionalised children's attention and positive affect: results from the BEIP study', *Journal of Child Psychology and Psychiatry* 50(3), 2009, 246–53

8. *For the 2007 meta-analysis covering studies on international adoption, see* M. H. Van Ijzendoorn, M. J. Bakermans-Kranenburg and F. Juffer, 'Plasticity of growth in height, weight, and head circumference: meta-analytic evidence of massive catch-up after international adoption', *Journal of Developmental and Behavioural Pediatrics* 28(4), 2007, 334–43

9. Bucharest Early Intervention Project, op. cit.

10. *For the 2007 Harvard study showing that children from institutions who were fostered at an early age fared better than those taken out later, see* C. A. Nelson III, C. H. Zeanah, N. A. Fox, P. J. Marshall, A. T. Smyke and D. Guthrie, 'Cognitive recovery in socially deprived young children: the Bucharest Early Intervention Project', *Science*, 318(5,858), 2007, 1,937–40

11. *For the 2004 UNICEF statistic, see* C. A. Nelson, 'A neurobiological perspective on early human deprivation', *Child Development Perspectives* 1(1), 2007, 13–18

12. *For the 2006 statistics of children living without available care-givers, visit* http://www.crin.org/docs/PPT%20BEIP%20Group.pdf (accessed 28 October 2009)

13. *For the 2005 study showing that oxytocin levels rose on playing in American children but not in Romanian orphans, see* A. B. Wismer Fries, T. E. Ziegler, J. R. Kurian, S. Jacoris and S. D. Pollack, 'Early experience in humans is associated with changes in neuropeptides critical for regulating social behaviour', *Proceedings of the National Academy of Sciences USA* 102, 2005, 17,237–40

14. *For the 2008 report on infant massage and vagus nerve activity, see* T. Field and M. Diego, 'Vagal activity, early growth and emotional development', *Infant Behaviour and Development* 31(3), 2008, 361–73

15. *For the study comparing the brains of 41 murderers with 41 controls, see* A. Raine, M. Buchsbaum and L. LaCasse, 'Brain abnormalities in murderers indicated by PET', *Biological Psychiatry* 42, 1997, 495–508

16. Sue Gerhardt, *Why Love Matters*, Routledge, New York, 2004

17. Ibid.

CHAPTER 11: COUNTING BLESSINGS

1. *For the 2003 study of blessings vs burdens, see* R. A. Emmons and M. E. McCullouch, 'Counting blessings versus burdens: an experimental investigation of gratitude and subjective well-being in daily life', *Journal of Personality and Social Psychology* 84(2), 2003, 377–89

2. *For the study using daily gratitude exercises, see* ibid.

3. *For the study with patients who had neuromuscular diseases, see* ibid.

4. *For the study where participants wrote and delivered a gratitude letter, see* Martin E. P. Seligman, *Authentic Happiness*, Nicholas Brealey, Boston, 2003

5. *For the 2005 study where participants did a gratitude exercise either once or three times a week for six weeks, see* S. Lyubomirsky, K. M. Sheldon and D. Schkade, 'Pursuing happiness: the architecture of sustainable change', *Review of General Psychology. Special Issue: Positive Psychology* 9(2), 2005, 111–31

6. *For the 1991 study that showed that thinking about an event over and over again reduced its impact, see* H. R. Arkes, L. E. Boehm and G. Xu, 'Determinants of judged validity', *Journal of Experimental Social Psychology* 27, 1991, 576–605

7. *For the 30-year optimists vs pessimists study, see* T. Maruta, R. C. Colligan, M. Malinchoc and K. P. Offord, 'Optimists vs pessimists: survival rate among medical patients over a 30-year period', *Mayo Clinic Proceedings* 75, 2000, 140–3

8. *For the 2002 Yale study that found that positivity extended life by 7.5 years, see* B. R. Levy, M. D. Slade, S. R. Kunkel and S. V. Kasl, 'Longevity increased by positive self-perceptions of ageing', *Journal of Personality and Social Psychology* 83(2), 2002, 261–70

9. *For the study of AIDS patients and attitude, see* G. M. Reed, M. E. Kemeny, S. E. Taylor, H.–Y. J. Wang and B. R. Visscher, 'Realistic acceptance as a predictor of decreased survival time in gay men with AIDS', *Health Psychology* 13, 1994, 299–307

10. *For the nun study, see* D. D. Danner, D. A. Snowdon and W. V. Friesen, 'Positive emotions in early life and longevity: findings from the nun study', *Journal of Personality and Social Psychology* 80(5), 2001, 804–13

11. *For the 2009 study about gratitude and sleep quality, see* A. M. Wood, S. Joseph, J. Lloyd and S. Atkins, 'Gratitude influences sleep through the mechanism of pre-sleep cognitions', *Journal of Psychosomatic Research* 66(1), 2009, 43–8

12. Robert A. Emmons, *Thanks: How the New Science of Gratitude Can Make You Happier*, Houghton Mifflin Harcourt, 2007

13. *For the 2008 study of 221 sixth- and seventh-grade students, see* J. J. Froh, W. J. Sefick and R. A. Emmons, 'Counting blessings in early adolescents: an experimental study of gratitude and subjective well-being', *Journal of School Psychology* 46, 2008, 213–33

14. *For the 'five things they don't have but wish they had' study, see* R. A. Emmons and M. E. McCullouch, 'Counting blessings versus burdens: an experimental investigation of gratitude and subjective well-being in daily life', *Journal of Personality and Social Psychology* 84(2), 2003, 377–89

15. *For the study on the effects of making comparisons on satisfaction, see* Emmons, 2007, op. cit.

16. Melody Beattie, *The Language of Letting Go*, Hazelden Information and Educational Services, Center City, Minnesota, 1990

17. *For a study on positive recall bias, see* P. C. Watkins, D. L. Grimm and R. Kolts, 'Counting your blessings: positive memories among grateful persons', *Current Psychology* 23(1), 2004, 52–67

18. *For the 'Big Sister Week' study, see* S. B. Algoe, J. Haidt and S. L. Gable, 'Beyond reciprocity: gratitude and relationships in everyday life', *Emotion* 8 (3), 2008, 425–9

19. *For the study of 700 newly-wed couples and the 5:1 r ratio, visit* http://www.udreview.com/news/prof-calcu' successful-marriage-1.831210 (accessed 29 Octobe

20. *For Robert Emmon's study of viewing life as a gift producing as much benefit as a standard gratitude exercise, see* Emmons, 2007, op. cit.

21. *For the 2004 study linking gratitude with depression, see* Watkins, Grimm and Kolts, op. cit.

22. *For a mention of the twin studies and the link between low gratitude and depression, see* Emmons, 2007, op. cit.

23. *For the study where heart attack patients saw benefits from their heart attack, see* G. Affleck, H. Tennen, S. Croog and S. Levine, 'Casual attribution, perceived benefits, and morbidity after a heart attack: an 8-year study', *Journal of Consultation and Clinical Psychology* 5(1), 1987, 29–35

24. *For the study of 3,000 patients with coronary blockages who counted their blessings, see* Dr Mimi Guarneri, *The Heart Speaks*, Simon & Schuster Inc., 2006

25. *For the study linking less pain with gratitude, see* Emmons, 2007, op. cit.

26. Norman Cousins, *Anatomy of an Illness*, W. W. Norton & Company, Inc., New York, 1979

27. *For the study where volunteers who watched humorous films had greatest pain tolerance, see* M. Weisenberg, T. Raz and T. Hener, 'The influence of film-induced mood on pain perception', *Pain* 76(3), 1998, 365–75

28. *For the gratitude and Alzheimer's account, see* Emmons, 2007, op. cit.

29. *For the 2008 'What if it never happened?' study, see* M. Koo, T. D. Wilson, S. B. Algoe and D. T. Gilbert, 'It's a wonderful life: mentally subtracting positive events improves people's affective states, contrary to their affective forecasts', *Journal of Personality and Social Psychology* 95(5), 2008, 1,217–24

CHAPTER 12: **LETTING GO OF THE PAST**

1. *For a mention of the study where revenge on unfaithful part-ners might sometimes be beneficial, see* G. Easterbrook, 'Forgiveness is good for your health', at http://www.beliefnet.com/Health/2002/03/Forgiveness-Is-Good-For-Your-Health.aspx (accessed 29 October 2009)

2. Immaculée Ilibagiza, *Left to Tell*, Hay House, London, 2006

3. *For the Northern Ireland HOPE project, see* F. M. Luskin and Reverend B. Bland, 'Stanford-Northern Ireland HOPE 1 project', 2000, http://www.learningtoforgive.com/research.htm (accessed 18 September 2009)

4. *For the HOPE 2 project, see* F. M. Luskin and Reverend B. Bland, 'Stanford-Northern Ireland HOPE 2 project', 2001, http://www.learningtoforgive.com/research.htm (accessed 18 September 2009)

5. *For the 2005 study of 55 students with unresolved interpersonal hurts, see* F. M. Luskin, K. Ginzburg and C. E. Thoresen, 'The effect of forgiveness training on psychosocial factors in college age adults', *Humboldt Journal of Social Relations. Special Issue: Altruism, Intergroup Apology and Forgiveness: Antidote for a Divided World* 29(2), 2005, 163–84

6. *For the Stanford study of 259 patients, see* A. H. Harris, F. M. Luskin, S. V. Benisovich, S. Standard, J. Bruning, S. Evans and C. Thoresen, 'Effects of group forgiveness intervention on perceived stress, state and trait anger, symptoms of stress, self-reported health and forgiveness (Stanford Forgiveness Project)', *Journal of Clinical Psychology* 62(6), 2006, 715–33

7. *For the comparison of 20 individuals in happy relationships compared with 20 individuals in troubled relationships, see* J. Lewis and J. Adler, 'Forgive and let live', *Newsweek*, September 27, 2004

8. *For the 1992 University of Wisconsin study that found that forgiveness improved blood flow to the heart, see* R. D. Enright, E. A. Gassin and C. Wu, 'Forgiveness: a developmental view', *Journal of Moral Education* 21, 1992, 99–114

9. *For the 2001 study where 71 people thought of hurtful memories or grudges, see* C. V. O. Witvliet, T. E. Ludwig and K. L. Vander Laan, 'Granting forgiveness or harbouring grudges: implications for emotion, physiology, and health', *Psychological Science* 121, 2001, 117–23

10. *For the 2007 study of 99 participants and heart recovery after stress, see* J. P. Friedberg, S. Suchday and D. V. Shelov, 'The impact of forgiveness on cardiovascular reactivity and recovery', *International Journal of Psychophysiology* 65(2), 2007, 87–94

11. *For the 2003 study of the heart attack patients who went through the 10-hour course in forgiveness, see* M. Waltman, D. Russell and R. Enright, 'Research study suggests forgiving attitude may be beneficial to the heart', Paper presented at the American Psychosomatic Society Annual Meeting, March 5–8, Phoenix, Arizona. *Visit* http://www.psychosomatic.org/media_ctr/press/annual/2003/07.htm to read about the study (accessed 29 October 2009)

12. *For the 2006 study of 25 hypertensive patients with high anger levels, see* D. Tibbits, G. Ellis, C. Piramelli, F. M. Luskin and R. Lukman, 'Hypertension reduction through forgiveness training', *Journal of Pastoral Care and Counselling* 60(1–2), 2006, 27–34

13. *For the study of the people in the financial services industry, see* F. M. Luskin, R. Aberman and A. E. deLorenzo, Sr, 'The training of emotional competence in financial services advisors', 2004, http://www.learningtoforgive.com/research.htm (accessed 18 September 2009)

14. *The quote from Jim La Rue was obtained from* http://www. signon-sandiego.com/uniontrib/20080816/news_1c16forgivem.html (accessed 29 October 2009)

15. *The quote from the Australian prime minister was obtained from* http://www.pm.gov.au/node/5952 (accessed 9 November 2009)

16. *For the study of religious versus non-religious based forgiveness counselling, see* M. S. Rye and K. I. Pargament, 'Forgiveness and romantic relationships in college: can it heal the wounded heart?', *Journal of Clinical Psychology* 58(4), 2002, 419–41

17. *For the 2006 study where people wrote about the benefits of transgressions, see* M. E. McCulloch, L. M. Root and A. D. Cohen, 'Writing about the benefits of an interpersonal transgression facilitates forgiveness', *Journal of Consulting and Clinical Psychology* 74(5), 2006, 887–97

18. *For the 'Time heals' study, see* M. J. Wohl and A. L. McGrath, 'The perception that time heals all wounds: temporal distance affects willingness to forgive following an interpersonal transgression', *Personality and Social Psychology Bulletin* 33(7), 2007, 1,023–35

CHAPTER 13: THE EVOLUTION OF KINDNESS

1. *For a description of Barbara Fredrickson's 'Broaden and Build' theory and the study where participants watched films to bring out positive emotions or fear or sadness, see* Barbara L. Fredrickson, PhD, *Positivity*, Crown Publishers, New York, 2009

2. *For play replacing conflict in chimpanzees, see* F. B. M. de Wall and A. van Roosmalen, 'Reconciliation and consolation among chimpanzees', *Behavioural Ecology and Sociobiology* 5, 1979, 55–66

3. *Frans de Waal was quoted in* E. O'Connor, 'Forgiveness heals the heart, research hints', 20 May 1999, http://www.cnn.com/HEALTH/9905/20/forgiveness/

4. Charles Darwin, *On the Origin of Species by Means of Natural Selection*, John Murray, London, 1859

5. *For a reference to the 500-million-year age of the oxytocin gene, visit* http://en.wikipedia.org/wiki/Oxytocin

6. *For a description of Paul Ekman's study of the Foré, see* Dacher Keltner, *Born to Be Good: The Science of a Meaningful Life*, Norton, New York, 2009

7. Ibid.

8. *For the 2009 study on emotional contagion and empathy, see* E. Hayfield, R. L. Rapson and Y. E. Le, 'Emotional Contagion and Empathy' in J. Decety & W. Ickes (eds), *The Social Neuroscience of Empathy*, MIT, Cambridge, MA, 2009

9. *For the 2006 study of pupil sizes, see* N. A. Harrison, T. Singer, P. Rotshtein, *et al.*, 'Pupillary contagion: central mechanisms engaged in sadness processing', *Social Cognitive and Affective Neuroscience* 1, 2006, 5–17

10. *For the 2007 study of the AVPR1a gene, see* A. Knafo, S. Israel, A. Darvasi, R. Bacgner-Melman, F. Uzefovsky, L. Cohen, E. Feldman, E. Lerer, E. Laiba, Y. Raz, L. Nemanov, I. Gritsenko, C. Dina, G. Agam, B. Dean, G. Bornstein and R. P. Ebstein, 'Individual differences in allocation of funds in the Dictator Game associated with length of the arginine vasopressin 1a receptor RS3 promoter region and correlations between RS3 length and hippocampal mRNA', *Genes Brain Behaviour* 7(3), 2007, 266–75

11. *In the 2009 study of the SNPs of the oxytocin receptor gene, see* S. Israel, E. Lerer, I. Shalev, F. Uzefovsky, M. Riebold, E.

Laiba, R. Bacher-Melman, A. Maril, G. Bornstein, A. Knafo and R. P. Ebstein, 'The oxytocin receptor (OXTR) contributes to prosocial fund allocations in the Dictator Game and the social value orientations task', *PLoS ONE* 4(5), 2009, e5535

12. For the 2009 study linking the oxytocin receptor gene with empathy, visit http://www.eurekalert.org/pub_releases/2009-11/osu-slg111209.php (accessed 23 November 2009)

13. *For the 2005 study of the SNPs of the dopamine receptor gene, see* R. Bachner-Melman, I. Gritsenko, L. Nemanov, A. H. Zohar, C. Dina and R. P. Ebstein, 'Dopaminergic polymorphisms associated with self-report measures of human altruism: a fresh phenotype for the dopamine D4 receptor', *Molecular Psychiatry* 10, 2005, 333–5

14. *For the statistic of 70 per cent of people giving away 40–50 per cent of the money, see* E. Fehr and K. M. Schmidt, 'A theory of fairness, competition, and cooperation', *Quarterly Journal of Economics* 114, 1999, 817–68

15. *For a description of the study where participants took painful electric shocks for each other, see* Keltner, op. cit.

CHAPTER 14: KINDNESS TOWARDS OURSELVES

1. *For the 2006 study where people were found to be 30 per cent more narcissistic, see* J. Twenge, *Generation Me: Why Today's Young Americans Are More Confident, Assertive, Entitled – And More Miserable Than Ever Before*, Free Press, New York, 2006

2. *For the 2005 study where students high on self-compassion were compared with students low on self-compassion, see* K. Neff, Y. Hsieh and K. Dejitterat, 'Self-compassion, achievement goals, and coping with academic failure', *Self and Identity* 4, 2005, 263–87

3. *For the 2007 study where self-compassion was investigated in different situations, see* M. R. Leary, E. B. Tate, A. B. Allen, C. E. Adams and J. Hancock, 'Self-compassion and reactions to unpleasant self-relevant events: the implications of treating oneself kindly', *Journal of Personality and Social Psychology* 92(5), 2007, 887–904

THE 21-DAY KINDNESS CHALLENGE

1. Amelia Earhart, http://www.ameliaearhart.com/about/quotes. html (accessed 9 November 2009)

RESOURCES

The following are books that you might enjoy that are related to some of the material in the individual chapters of this book:

Melody Beattie, *The Language of Letting Go*, Hazelden Information and Educational Services, Center City, Minnesota, 1990

Diane Berke, *The Gentle Smile: Practicing Oneness in Daily Life*, Crossroad Publishing Company, New York, 1995

Will Bowen, *A Complaint-Free World*, Doubleday, New York, 2007

Norman Cousins, *Anatomy of an Illness*, W. W. Norton & Company, Inc., New York, 1979

Jerry A. Coyne, *Why Evolution is True*, Oxford University Press, Oxford, 2009

Charles Darwin, *The Expression of the Emotions in Man and Animals*, ed. Paul Ekman, Fontana Press, London, 1999 (200th anniversary edition)

Richard Dawkins, *The Selfish Gene*, Oxford University Press, Oxford, 1976

Norman Doidge, MD, *The Brain That Changes Itself*, Viking Penguin, New York, 2007

Robert A. Emmons, *Thanks: How the New Science of Gratitude Can Make You Happier*, Houghton Mifflin Harcourt, Boston, 2007

Piero Ferrucci, *The Power of Kindness: The Unexpected Benefits of Leading a Compassionate Life*, Jeremy P. Tarcher/Penguin, New York, 2006

Barbara L. Fredrickson, PhD, *Positivity*, Crown Publishers, New York, 2009

Sue Gerhardt, *Why Love Matters: How Affection Shapes a Baby's Brain*, Routledge, East Sussex, 2004

Paul Gilbert, *The Compassionate Mind*, Constable & Robinson Ltd, London, 2009

Dr Mimi Guarneri, *The Heart Speaks*, Fusion Press, London, 2006

David R. Hamilton, PhD, *How Your Mind Can Heal Your Body*, Hay House, London, 2008

Mark Henderson, *50 Genetic Ideas You Really Need to Know*, Quercus, London, 2008

Immaculée Ilibagiza, *Left to Tell*, Hay House, London, 2006

Dacher Keltner, *Born to Be Good: The Science of a Meaningful Life*, Norton, New York, 2009

Richard Layard, *Happiness: Lessons from a New Science*, Penguin, New York, 2005

Thomas Lewis, Fari Amini, and Richard Lannon, *A General Theory of Love*, Vintage, New York, 2001

Fred Luskin, *Forgive for Good*, HarperSanFrancisco, 2002

Allan Luks, *The Healing Power of Doing Good*, iUniverse.com, Lincoln, 1991

T. G. Plante and C. E. Thorensen, *Spirit, Science, and Health: How the Spiritual Mind Fuels Physical Wellness*, Praeger Publishers, Westport, 2007

Random Acts of Kindness, Editors of Conari Press, Conari Press, San Francisco, 1993

Allan N. Schore, *Affect Regulation and the Origin of the Self: The Neurobiology of Emotional Development*, Lawrence Erlbaum Associates, Inc., New Jersey, 1994

Martin E. P. Seligman, *Authentic Happiness*, Nicholas Brealey, Boston, 2003

J. Twenge, *Generation Me: Why Today's Young Americans Are More Confident, Assertive, Entitled – And More Miserable Than Ever Before*, Free Press, New York, 2006

Danny Wallace, *Random Acts of Kindness*, Ebury Press, London, 2004

INDEX

JOIN THE HAY HOUSE FAMILY

As the leading self-help, mind, body and spirit publisher in the UK, we'd like to welcome you to our family so that you can enjoy all the benefits our website has to offer.

EXTRACTS from a selection of your favourite author titles

COMPETITIONS, PRIZES & SPECIAL OFFERS Win extracts, money off, downloads and so much more

LISTEN to a range of radio interviews and our latest audio publications

CELEBRATE YOUR BIRTHDAY An inspiring gift will be sent your way

LATEST NEWS Keep up with the latest news from and about our authors

ATTEND OUR AUTHOR EVENTS Be the first to hear about our author events

iPHONE APPS Download your favourite app for your iPhone

HAY HOUSE INFORMATION Ask us anything, all enquiries answered

join us online at **www.hayhouse.co.uk**

292B Kensal Road, London W10 5BE
T: 020 8962 1230 E: info@hayhouse.co.uk

We hope you enjoyed this Hay House book.
If you would like to receive a free catalogue featuring additional
Hay House books and products, or if you would like information
about the Hay Foundation, please contact:

Hay House UK Ltd
292B Kensal Road • London W10 5BE
Tel: (44) 20 8962 1230; Fax: (44) 20 8962 1239
www.hayhouse.co.uk

***

Published and distributed in the United States of America by:
Hay House, Inc. • PO Box 5100 • Carlsbad, CA 92018-5100
Tel: (1) 760 431 7695 or (1) 800 654 5126;
Fax: (1) 760 431 6948 or (1) 800 650 5115
www.hayhouse.com

***

Published and distributed in Australia by:
Hay House Australia Ltd • 18/36 Ralph Street • Alexandria, NSW 2015
Tel: (61) 2 9669 4299, Fax: (61) 2 9669 4144
www.hayhouse.com.au

***

Published and distributed in the Republic of South Africa by:
Hay House SA (Pty) Ltd • PO Box 990 • Witkoppen 2068
Tel/Fax: (27) 11 467 8904
www.hayhouse.co.za

***

Published and distributed in India by:
Hay House Publishers India • Muskaan Complex • Plot No.3
B-2 • Vasant Kunj • New Delhi - 110 070
Tel: (91) 11 41761620; Fax: (91) 11 41761630
www.hayhouse.co.in

***

Distributed in Canada by:
Raincoast • 9050 Shaughnessy St • Vancouver, BC V6P 6E5
Tel: (1) 604 323 7100
Fax: (1) 604 323 2600

***

Sign up via the Hay House UK website to receive the Hay House
online newsletter and stay informed about what's going on with your
favourite authors. You'll receive bimonthly announcements
about discounts and offers, special events, product highlights,
free excerpts, giveaways, and more!
www.hayhouse.co.uk